Healing
with the Energy of the
Chakras

by

Ambika Wauters

THE CROSSING PRESS
FREEDOM, CALIFORNIA

For information on bulk purchases or group discounts for this and other Crossing Press titles, please contact our Special Sales Manager at 800–777–1048.

Visit our Web site on the Internet at: www.crossingpress.com

Healing and medicine are two very different disciplines, and the law requires the following disclaimer. The information in this book is not medicine but healing, and it does not constitute medical advice. In case of serious illness consult the practitioner of your choice.

Library of Congress Cataloging-in-Publication Data

Wauters, Ambika.
    [Ambika's guide to healing and wholeness]
    Healing with the energy of the chakras / by Ambika Wauters.
        p. cm.
    Originally published in 1993 under the title: Ambika's guide to healing and wholeness
    ISBN 0-89594-906-7 (pbk.)
    1. Mental healing. 2. Chakras. 3. Healing--Miscellanea.
    I. Title.
RZ401.W38   1998
615.8'52--dc21   98-26907
                                            CIP

This book is dedicated to Janetta and Sequoia,
spirit guides who illuminated the process of formulating this book.

To my grandmother, Ester Lewin Ferer, whose memory I cherish.

And to Charlie Moritz whose love and strength of heart
help me to open to my heart.

Acknowledgments

I would like to thank my friends and teachers who have so graciously assisted me on my path.

Gaynor and Edward Grimshaw and their family encouraged and helped me come to England and redefine my goals in life. They gave help at every level, easing the transition to new territory, both inner and outer. Their love, encouragement, and support helped me to plant new roots. My first teacher in Bioenergetics and massage was Dr. Alexis Johnson. After a long absence from Finca La Follenca Growth Centre in Southern Spain, she opened her heart and her home in New York to me so that I could be with my sister during her struggle with leukemia. Thanks to Paul Charles Collins for the use of his computer. My good friends, Sue Bell and Sandy Cotter, gave love and support all along the way.

H. W. L. Poonja of Lucknow, India, is my spiritual teacher. His love and teachings sustained me through upheaval and change which brought me to grater realization about the Source—that we are always protected and guided.

The main part of this book has come out of the workshops I have offered on Color Healing and the Chakras. I wish to thank all those who participated. Every participant has affirmed for me the gentle nature of this work.

Contents

Preface

What Are Chakras?

Chakras are swirling wheels of light and color—vortices of flowing energy which sustain us energetically, adding to and vitalizing our life-force.

As an essential element of the human energy system, they are like a ladder of love, leading us higher and higher to greater quantities and more refined qualities of love. At an energetic level they are channels through which vital energy must pass in order to nourish and maintain physical, emotional, mental, and spiritual life as we know it to be.

Chakras focus the confluence of energy streaming down on us from the cosmos and up from the depths of the earth. They bloom and radiate when stimulated by specific sounds, colors, and scents, and are responsive to positive and negative thoughts and emotions. As we grow and develop throughout our lives our chakras will open and expand to allow more refined energy to enter our systems, and this will be reflected in the degree to which we are truly alive, and in our happiness and stability.

Each chakra represents a distinct level of development and awareness. The Root Chakra, which is located at the base of our spine, gives us our grounding in life and embodies such qualities as patience, constancy, commitment, and stability. The Crown Chakra, which is the polar opposite of the Root Chakra, connects us to the spirit within and around us. It gives guidance, protection, and a deepening sense of beauty and healing.

Energy follows thought. Within the chakra system there can be dysfunction, and this may even lead to disease when thoughts about oneself or about life become chronically negative. Fear and doubt undermine our sense of emotional well-being. At an energetic level these negative thoughts corrode our vitality and good health. They disempower us and leave us at the mercy of external circumstance. Working with this book and developing an understanding of the emotional components of the chakras can give you a healthy framework for moving past your emotional blocks. It will help deepen your understanding of physical dysfunction and generally improve your health and lifestyle, leaving you more in harmony with your greatest joy and in tune with your higher self.

Self-Healing

We are, I feel, at the point in the history of our planet where we must grasp the importance of personal development and accept the need for transformation from negativity and exploitation to positive and affirmative attitudes towards life. For centuries we have projected our power into institutions, governments, doctors, and teachers to make our lives work for us. Yet these very systems which we have trusted to do the job of looking after us are in the process of change. Increasingly we are being asked to look within ourselves for the solutions and answers to our well-being and survival. When we begin this process of self-help we open the channels for healing to happen and this is experience as greater happiness and contentment, as well as the ability to make positive decisions. In so doing we inevitably achieve greater degrees of physical and mental health.

Spirit is universal. It flows within and outside us. We are all part and parcel of one and the same energy. All solutions to the problems posed in living a balanced and happy life are there to be found inside every one of us. This book is aimed at helping you discover your unique spiritual qualities and enhancing the light within you. It is a self-help program intended to give you guidelines and a framework within which to explore and understand more about how your energetic system responds to thoughts and expression. This, in turn, may help you to shift your perceptions about who you are and what life can offer you. It may awaken you to your real purpose in being here on the planet at this time. I hope it will open you to the possibility of deepening levels of joy and love.

Introduction

My introduction to energy work started over twenty years ago when I participated in group therapy sessions in London. Facilitators often spoke about "energy." Then it sounded like something mystical which was only perceptible to very sensitive people. What they described, after all, was something which other people could not see. I was intrigued to know exactly what it was these people saw and felt. I thought, at the time, that I might have the aptitude for this type of energy work myself.

This book comes out of many years of personal and professional experience of clearing negative patterns and the resistance to change. As I pursued my own personal growth and development I did indeed become much more sensitive to energy. It seemed that the more I was able to confront the personal issues which blocked my vitality the more sensitized I became to the realm of subtle energy. Since those early days in London I have studied and trained with many people experienced in energy work. I have also studied yoga, martial arts, dance, meditation, and massage, as well as Cranial Sacral Therapy and Homeopathy. These pursuits have all given me a greater well-being and a deeper sense of self. I am still learning to transform negative pull into positive, life-affirming states which can release blocked tension and rebalance energy.

You don't need to be psychic or a healer to gain awareness from this book. My hope is that it will go some way towards bridging the gap between therapy and healing; and that you will gain more health, aliveness, and happiness in your life through the insights you find for yourself in this book.

In approaching our emotional blocks and negativity towards life, with a view to releasing them, we cannot help but empower ourselves. The more we do this ourselves through the process of taking responsibility for who we are the greater our total sense of being alive. In turn our increased vitality and energy give us the opportunity to be joyfully creative.

Through releasing our deep tension and negative holding patterns we become more involved participants in life. Change and adaptability are both important prerequisites for good health. The energy that both of these demand is readily and naturally available to us without any need to resort to either stimulants or drugs.

When we look at our fears, and let go of those doubts and attitudes which can block the life-force, we then make that energy available for our creativity and well-being; energy which, though subtle, is still quite measurable and understandable.

I hope this book will give you a greater understanding of yourself and that you will find it fun as well as informative. Putting this gentle, non-intrusive work into practice may also help to heal deep wounds to the psyche and soul. The chakras and their colors carry within them all the components we need for our higher evolution. As we grow and evolve out of the primordial mass and individuate into responsible and creative human beings, so we are asked to clarify, refine, and develop ourselves. If we are blocked at some level (and which of us isn't?) it is useful to refer to the chakras and colors as tools for understanding more about what our negative issues may be, and exactly what qualities we may need to call on for our own transformation. Life will always present an incessant flow of experiences and situations to us, giving us the opportunity to know and recognize the depths of who we are. An understanding of energy and the emotional framework in which chakras and color function can help to support and nurture us through stress and crisis. This knowledge has certainly helped me, during times of emotional turmoil and chaos, to find a spiritual framework in which to hold my life experiences so that I could safely release old thought patterns which impeded my growth.

Within this framework of the chakras we are offered the possibility of self-healing; it is a guide to how energy flows, becomes blocked and congested, and offers a means whereby we can choose to open ourselves to greater quantities and more refined qualities of spiritual energy. Without judgment, self-reproach, or the risk of over-identification with our feelings we are given an emotional blueprint of ourselves which guides us towards being more positive, energetic, and fulfilled.

Part One
Healing with Color and Energy

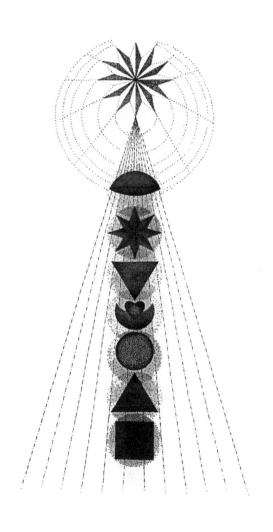

Chakras: An Introduction

We have inherited the chakras and their colors from yoga and Chinese medicine. These systems have been highly refined and developed over thousands of years in the East. Today, in our modern world, we can make use of this system to heal our emotional blocks and the limiting attitudes which stand in the way of our well-being and development. Chakras studied purely and simply as an esoteric science add up to no more than a dry and brittle skeleton. They come to life when we add the flesh and blood of emotions and when we can then relate them to our daily life. When we understand how chakras relate to our emotional harmony they become something which we can grasp and use to benefit our health and well-being. Chakras are, in a sense, an evolutionary ladder towards a higher consciousness. They offer us the possibility of increased self-awareness, growth, and maturity if we wish to use them as a framework for our development.

Colors are also a component of the chakras. They can be used as a healing tool to soothe, stimulate, or balance energy. Color Therapy is an ancient form of healing, using the visible spectrum of light to help the healing and recovery of the body and spirit.

Understanding Chakras

The work *chakra* comes from the Sanskrit and means "wheel." Chakras are actually vortices of energy, spiraling up from the earth and down from the cosmos. Where these meet in the human energy system is just outside the surface of our physical bodies. We are enveloped in an energetic sheath known as the "aura." This envelope is similar to the layers of atmosphere which surround and protect the earth. Within the atmospheric strata are layers of energy which sustain and nourish life on this planet. Without these layers of energy it would be impossible for life to exist. There would be no oxygen to enable us to breathe. By analogy this is also true for the individual auric field. Without the envelope of energy which acts as a boundary for our individual existence there could not be physical life as we know it.

Chakras are not mystical. They are, in fact, an essential part of our bio-energy system. They enable us to gather, process, and release energy from the earth and from the atmosphere around us. They feed the life-force into our endocrine system which, in turn, stimulates and regulates our hormonal balance.

This energy which is channeled into our bodies is called the vital force in homeopathy; in the yogic system it is referred to as Prana, while Wilhelm Reich called it the Orgone Field. The chakras conduct and filter a constant flow of life-energy through us. What is so unique to this system is the gradation and refinement of energy available as we evolve through the chakras to higher levels of awareness, responsibility, and consciousness. As we evolve and develop, so each chakra opens and feeds that next level of development.

This book explores the nature of the seven major Chakras. These are: *the Root Chakra*, located at the base of the spine; *the Sacral Chakra*, located below the navel in the pelvis; *the Solar Plexus Chakra*, located just under the rib cage in the area of the stomach; *the Heart Chakra*, located in the mid chest; *the Throat Chakra*, located in the region of the neck; *the Brow Chakra*, found in the forehead, and *the Crown Chakra*, which sits on top of the head. (See the diagram on page 5.)

There are twenty-one minor chakras throughout the body. All the acupuncture points are chakras as well. As we evolve into higher and

3

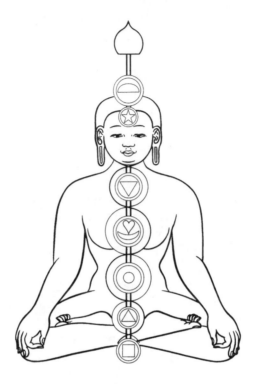

The symbols on this Buddha show where the chakras are located. In ascending order they are Root; Sacral; Solar Plexus; Heart; Throat; Brow; and Crown.

more refined levels of awareness and expand into cosmic consciousness we will develop new centers for processing even more rarefied energy. Chakras are the vessels which feed the dynamic, energetic system of life throughout our bodies.

Chakras are conductors of energy to all life-forms. It is believed that the mineral kingdom is made up of one chakra. The animal kingdom has three to four chakras. We are given all of these plus the transpersonal chakras which enable us to love, communicate, think, and reflect on God.

Having an Open Mind about Subtle Energy

What is being asked of us in exploring the realm of subtle energy is a willingness to go beyond our everyday believe system. We need to incorporate a different view of ourselves. We are energetic beings, not mechanical robots. With this understanding comes the need to realize the depths of our gentle and sensitive natures, and to honor the spiritual dimension within ourselves.

We are responsive to everything that happens around us, both internally and externally, throughout the planet and, for that matter, throughout the universe. Our minds act as filters for the vast number of stimuli which are bombarding our consciousness at any one time.

Meditation and massage, for instance, tune us into the inner realms of ourselves which contain our personal truths about how we are feeling. This is only a matter of connecting to the deep knowing without ourselves. Science is demonstrating that we are composed of the same submolecular substance from which the universe if built. Within our cellular structure is the genetic code distilled from all the experiences it has taken us to individuate into loving and conscious beings. We are beginning to learn that we are unlimited co-creators of the universe. We have within us the capacity to create our lives the way we would like them to be. The essential thing is to know who we are and what we need for our continued growth and development. We are all looking for ways to develop trust and faith that life will look after us and provide for our continued growth and survival. Chakras are a tool that can help develop that awareness.

I have had a strong feeling for a while now that if we heal ourselves of the blocks to our own life enhancement, we will simultaneously be healing the planet. This concept of "morphic resonance" is described in a story from one of my homeopathic teachers. She tells of a girl who had terrible problems completing a sentence. We were told that every time we completed a sentence we helped this girl to complete *her* sentences. We did this through our intention, which created a force field which this girl could unconsciously experience as a support for her problem.

The concept of morphic resonance also applies to the clearing of congested energy from the human energy system. No one is ever healed

5

alone. When one person is healed, all of us experience this at some deep level of our being. We are part of a greater whole, helping and supporting one another. As we decongest the energy which has blocked us and prevented the life-force within us from fully functioning, we free the collective energy within us all.

Through years of psychotherapeutic training and practice I have come to see that growth is a process which involves pain. Healing, to me, requires love. It is love which sustains, nurtures, and enhances life. Yet we still need the painful processes at times in our lives to allow us the quantum leaps in our development as human beings.

Through opening our hearts, releasing our emotions and forgiving, we free vital energy from our core. This energy has become imploded in the fiber of our cells and in our energetic field. We are all familiar with people who carry hatred in their hearts. They are unpleasant to be around and after spending time with them we feel tired and drained. The converse of that is being around lovers or people who are happy and contented with life. They offer us a glimpse of inner stability, ease, and joy. It is a pleasure to be around them. When the heart is open and free the dynamic life-force flows from the center of our being out to the whole of life. Transformation need not be harsh or dramatic. When we consciously choose change the universal life-force responds to our intentions. Working with the chakras is a gentle and unintrusive way of releasing energy from our systems. When that energy is liberated it can be used for our creativity and pleasure.

At our core we are creatures of light who want only acceptance, expression, and space to radiate. What is asked at this time on the planet is first to honor that light in ourselves and then to recognize it in one another. Chakras work with the colors of light which show us our own radiance. We are all a spectrum of color which reflects the One Light shining within us. It is my hope that in working with this book you may become more aware of your beauty, your grace, and your own unique expression of the life-force.

Working with Subtle Energy

Techniques for Working with Subtle Energy

This chapter gives you various techniques to transform energy blocked in the chakras. These techniques can help you balance energy. They are designed to redistribute and stabilize energy throughout your energy system.

Dysfunction in the Energy Field

Chakras become dysfunctional when they are congested with stale or stagnant energy. They can become overcharged through unexpressed emotions. Dysfunction can occur at the physical level. Here you could have a problem with circulation, inflammation, or underfunctioning of a system or organ. At the emotional level you may find that you are chronically low of spirit, or oversensitive or angry towards people or things. Mentally there may be lack of insight into problems. Rigid attitudes might reflect fear, doubt, or mistrust which dampen your enjoyment of life. By carefully and objectively looking at your life on these levels you will be able to assess which areas of your life need transforming. Look at the techniques in this section and gently feel your way into them. What is suitable for your needs at this moment? The techniques are subtle but have a powerful effect on your energetic system. You should feel freer and lighter as a result of working with the chakras and their colors.

The Techniques

The essence of this work lies in stimulating your energy system into activity and charging it with energy. Through these gentle and non-intrusive techniques, energy will start to move, and then be released. They will only release what is stuck on the surface of the chakras and work best if they are done in sequence. I suggest you begin with breathing and movement and follow this with meditation and massage. Always end this work by sealing off the energy in the chakras. This gives you balance and a wonderful sense of well-being.

In the workshops I offer on chakras and color I use aromatherapy oils to stimulate the chakras. I use brightly colored lights and play soothing music when I do the massage. I find it useful to have pictures of the chakras around when doing the meditation so that people can easily refer to the colors and symbols. Affirmations can also be very useful if and when you come to a negative state of mind or an uncomfortable block. You may wish to change your thinking about a situation or feeling which has come up. This can best be done by allowing the feeling to come into your consciousness, and giving it full space to be there without feeling wrong for experiencing it. Often unconscious feelings are the ones we did not allow ourselves to feel in the past because it wasn't permitted or we did not feel safe expressing them. If, for example, during the massage you begin to experience deep grief over the loss of someone or something which was very important in your life, then the feelings may start to flow through you in the form of deep sighs, tears, sobbing, or intense weeping. My suggestion is that you allow yourself to experience these feelings. You can then begin t heal the pain of that wound by reciting an affirmation over and over to yourself. A good one for this form of grief may be to say "*I am always connected by love to those I love and care for.*" This helps to release more imploded energy and starts the healing process.

The degree to which you can permit yourself to feel your feelings is the degree to which healing can happen for you in the form of release. This is how we gain inner peace and stability.

Subtle Energy Techniques

Breathing and Movement

In subtle energy work we use breathing and movement to energize the body. They create a current of activity which charges the energy field and stimulates the chakras. Every time we consciously breathe or move we are nourishing our energetic systems.

Breathing and movement increase the flow of the life-force. They help to release stale, stagnant energy which has imploded into the system. This process of release works right the way through from the grossest physical level to the most refined realms of subtle energy.

We all need fresh, clean air and enough movement to maintain discharge and release toxins which build up and accumulate in our blood. This can come from poor nutrition, lack of exercise, and long-standing emotional suppression. It is the same with the emotional energy system. Discharge comes when we release negative patterns and blocked feelings.

The development of such refined sciences as Yoga and Chinese medicine has taken thousands of years to perfect. They are based on an accurate understanding of energetic principles. These systems transform energy on all levels. They are designed to promote health by the systematic discharge of energy through breathing and movement. Anyone who practices Yoga or Tai Chi knows that immense feeling of well-being which follows a session. It can, however, become suppressive when people do not deal with their emotions. Often in therapy I ask clients to refrain from practices like Yoga or martial arts s that the suppressed feelings can begin to surface. This way, long-standing issues and negativity can be dealt with and a person is then free of them rather than run by them. I do feel that what sits in the unconscious runs us. Once we experience it we are free of it. In Homeopathy we stimulate the vital force to overcome suppression so that the patient can regain their natural state of balance and health.

Selecting Music to Work With

When you begin working with the subtle energy of the chakras I suggest you choose music which will inspire you to move freely. This may be something lively or rhythmical, flowing or poignant. What is important is that you choose music which expresses your feelings in the moment and which helps you start moving.

The Release Breath

Begin by taking a few deep breaths in through your nose and releasing your breath out through your mouth. The release of energy through your breath is the most important part of the respiration for this work. We are all holding on to emotions which block the flow of our energy. Breathing is the easiest way to release these blocked feelings. As long as we live the inspiration of air will occur automatically. There is nothing we have to do for this: it is a "given" in life. But the release of our breath is something we can consciously control. Breaking a particular emotional pattern begins by giving some resounding breaths out through your mouth. I often suggest to people that they *blow* their problems and pain out through their mouth. Empty the stale air from your lungs and let your breath begin to flow.

Utilizing Movement to Free Up Energy

The movements can be simple, repetitive, gentle, fast or slow. Start to let go of the tension in your neck, face, jaw, and shoulders. Bend, twist, jump, or do what feels good to free the physical body of its holding and restrictive patterns.

Take some deep breaths, release your tension, and allow the movement within you to find an outlet of expression.

When you have moved for a while start to focus your breathing into the lower part of your back, legs, and feet. You may find that after a while the movements slow down, the breathing becomes gentler, and you start to listen to its rhythmic patterns. Within these, you can often find an indication of what you would like to do next. As you focus on your breath you may find you wish to release a sound from your throat. Let this sound come out from your depths and b a part of the expression of how you are feeling at that moment. Doing this will automatically begin to release blocked emotional energy.

Doing this in front of a mirror will let you see how you move. Look carefully at yourself and see where you are open and where you restrict yourself. Allow yourself to love the image you see of yourself. Loving yourself exactly as you are helps to release fears, lack of confidence, and anxieties. Criticism only works to block your energy. Use an affirmation as you move to increase the flow of positive energy you are building up with the movement. This is a way of saying "yes" to yourself and affirming your unique expression of who you are.

Moving goes a long way to recovering a sense of joy in the body. It will take off layers of superficial tension you may be holding, and will make it much easier for you to progress to the next step in this process of working with subtle energy, meditation. You will be able to sit in a more relaxed, comfortable way and so be able to concentrate more easily. Breathing and movement are the first steps towards relaxation. They will make meditation and massage that much more pleasurable for you.

Chakras and Color Meditation

Meditation is a good tool for looking inside. It is a way of tuning in and listening to your depths. There are many different techniques for meditation. The one offered to you here has been developed to give you an awareness of energy centers.

This meditation will take you on a journey through your energetic system by introducing you to your chakras and their colors. It can open new dimensions of experience in the realms of subtle energy. It can help you to release tension and begin to stabilize your energy and emotions. It will show you where the energy centers are located in the body and put you in touch with any sensations, memories, and emotions associated with these centers.

Sitting Comfortably

To begin the chakra meditation find a comfortable place to sit. You may wish to sit in a chair which will support your back, or lie down on a firm surface to keep your spine straight. If you choose this, place a book 3–4 inches thick under your head to support your neck. Bend your knees and place your feet flat on the ground so you are resting semi-supine to take the strain off your lower back.

However you sit, make sure that your spine is straight and your head is sitting straight on your neck. This allows energy to move easily up and down your spine.

Breathing

Begin your meditation with some deeply releasing breaths to help you focus your awareness inside yourself.

As you focus your breathing, begin to release any tension you feel in your body. Search your body with your inner sense and feel for tension as you move your awareness through your feet and ankles, knees, hip joints, and lower back. Bring your awareness up along your spine, through your chest, and into the region of your heart. Now take your awareness into your neck and shoulders, and into your face, giving special attention to your jaw and behind your eyes and above your ears. These are all places where we hold tension.

The more relaxed you are in yourself the easier it will be to focus your awareness in the subtle realms of energy. You will be able to distinguish what tension you are holding on to and what energy is flowing freely through the chakras. You will also be able to differentiate between some of your emotions.

Experiencing Your Feelings

You will soon be able to differentiate between the hot and passionate feelings which sit in the belly. They may be aggression, anger, even rage. Humor and hilarity are very alive feelings which also rest in the belly. Anxiety sits in the stomach region and may have strong physical sensations such as tightness and constriction.

The cooler feelings of sorrow and sadness often lodge in the chest around the heart. Grief can pervade to affect the hands, fingers, shoulder joints, and the neck.

When you have feelings which are uncomfortable allow them space to be experienced. Breathe through them deeply, and fully release them with every exhalation. Trust yourself to be able to experience whatever comes up for you as you slowly and gently tune into yourself. Slowly and with time you can begin to release these blocks through your increased sensitivity and ability to transform energetic patterns with positive, affirmative thoughts.

If you find yourself overwhelmed with feelings it may be appropriate to cry. If you are very angry get up and move rather than suppress your feelings. You may wish to use your voice to shout or hit some cushions to release the tension. It makes it easier to sit quietly and concentrate if blocked emotions are first released. Be willing to move past your fears and to feel and express yourself.

Visualization

Throughout this meditation try visualizing the chakra symbols and the colors which relate to them. Imagine these forms and colors to have energy, heat, warmth, and sensations of pleasure. Look at the illustration on the cover which shows energy from the Source coming down and being assimilated through the chakras.

In the following section there are color meditations for each of the chakras. Again, use the color symbols to focus your awareness and stimulate your imagination. You may wish to hold some crystals to help focus the energy flow. Place your hands over the areas of the chakras in the beginning so that you can have a sense of where they are located. The quieter you are within yourself the more deeply your consciousness can penetrate your deep core.

Meditation for the Root Chakra

Sit quietly and take some deeply relaxing breaths. Allow your awareness to sink deep into your body. Feel yourself sitting in a chair or on the ground. Feel your feet and legs.

The Root Chakra is located at the bottom of the spine in the perineum. This chakra has one funnel, or channel, which is directed down towards the earth. The color which emanates from this center is red. Its form is that of a cube.

- Hold this image in your mind. Concentrate on intensifying the color and solidifying the form of the cube.

- Imagine the heat of this red cube moving through the base of your pelvis and down through your thighs, into your knees, calves, ankles, and out of the base of your feet.

- Visualize your bones, tissues, and cells. See them absorbing the energy of this red cube. As you take in this energy you are being strengthened throughout your body. You are absorbing vitality and life into every cell.

- Your whole being is energized by the life-force concentrated in this red cube.

- Concentrate on this image for a few moments of stillness and silence.

- Imagine a red cube located at the base of your spine.

- As you see this cube of energy radiating red light into your pelvis, legs, and feet, allow gravity to pull this energy down into the earth. You can feel the weight and density of this red cube as its energy is drawn down towards the center of the earth connecting you and energizing you.

- Soak in the vibration of this color and take it into your entire body. Feel the energy of this red cube pulsating in the base of your spine. It energizes your blood, bones, and muscles.

- The attributes which form the foundation of the red cube are: structure; stability; security; manifestation; patience; commitment; constancy; and order. Take a few moments to reflect on the meaning of these qualities in your life. They grow and develop in you each day, and help to form the cornerstone of your life. They support you in difficult times and ensure that you are well-grounded.

- Repeat to yourself:
  "I am safe and secure at all times."
  "I am open to expanding my awareness of life."
  "Life is good."
  "I have a strong foundation in life."

Practice will help you in this meditation. What you were unable to do yesterday becomes easier today. Be gentle and patient. The mind responds quickly to colors. The forms may take more concentration and time to visualize. They too can be instantly recalled with some attention.

Meditation for the Sacral Chakra

The location of the Sacral Chakra is two fingers down from your navel and two fingers in. It sits in the center of your pelvis. It radiates energy to the front and out of the back of your pelvis. The color of the Sacral Chakra is orange. The form is that of a pyramid.

- Visualize this center and imagine the pyramid having weight and substance. The weight of the pyramid brings your awareness down into your pelvis.

- The Sanskrit translation for this chakra means "my home," or "my sweetness." Knowing this will help you to focus your awareness here. This is where you can be at home within yourself. It is a safe, warm, nourishing place to be. As you rest here you become energized and vitalized. At the same time you are deeply relaxed. This is what is referred to as being centered.

- Now visualize orange light radiating from the center of the pyramid. See it moving through your genitals, the floor of your pelvis, into your intestines, bladder, and kidneys. As the orange light moves through you it is sweeping away disease, congestion, inflammations, fear, anxiety, and other tension which remains in this area.

- This orange light gives you a deep feeling of well-being. You can allow the sensation of pleasure and warmth to move through your belly.

  Your sense of ease and relaxation are expanding. You are in harmony with your vision of yourself. You are enough. You have everything you need to be happy now. As you visualize this radiant orange light shining from your pelvis take a deep breath and say to yourself, *"I trust life."* Repeat this to yourself several times.

- The attributes which form the four sides of this orange pyramid are: well-being; pleasure; sexuality; and abundance/prosperity.

- Know now that these qualities are growing stronger in you every day. Your sense of who you are is growing every day. Your willingness to allow pleasure and fun into your life is expanding every moment.
  Remember:
  "Who I am is enough."
  "What I do is enough."
  "What I have is enough."

- When you feel there is enough orange light for your cells, tissues, and organs to be completely nourished let the orange light radiate from within the pyramid. Begin to extend this light out of your body. Imagine this orange light now embraces the red cube within it.

- Take a few deep release breaths and allow yourself to feel whole and complete just as you are in this moment.
  Now say to yourself:
  "All is well in my universe."

Meditation for the Solar Plexus Chakra

Bring your awareness up to your solar plexus just under the sternum where your stomach is situated. This is a very sensitive spot of the body. It may be tense, sore, or feel congested. Take several deep releasing breaths and begin to relax, focusing your awareness into this area.

The color of this chakra is yellow. The form is a sphere.

- Begin to imagine this golden, yellow sphere glowing in your stomach. It is energizing and feeding all your vital organs. Focus it in your liver and gallbladder located on the right side of your body. Let this light decongest any tension there.

- Now move it into the stomach region and let the yellow sphere warm your stomach and soothe away the tension. Expand the light to the left side of your body and let it energize your pancreas and spleen. Now focus it into your lungs and heart. There is a lot of energy concentrated in this area of your body. It can be channeled for your relaxation, pleasure, and health.

- The attributes of this yellow sphere are: self-respect; integrity; self-worth; good judgment; decision-making; and personal power. These qualities are growing and expanding in you daily. They enhance your sense of who you are and let you feel good about yourself.

  Tension is beginning to melt away as the warmth from this yellow sphere soothes and relaxes you.

- Take a deep breath and release any remaining tension in your solar plexus.

- Keep imagining this golden, yellow light radiating through your organs, detoxifying, cleansing, and stimulating your energy. When you feel that you have utilized this energy for your own benefit begin to let the golden yellow sphere filter out from the front of your solar plexus as well as from the area of the spine behind your stomach.

- Imagine this yellow light embracing the orange pyramid and the red cube. You now feel rooted in life with a strong sense of well-being and of your own worth.

- Take a deep, releasing breath and say to yourself:
  "I am worthy."
  "I am worth my weight in gold."
  "I am worthy of my own self-love."

- It is time to rest, relax, and stop pushing so hard. It is time to feel good about your own worth as a person. This sense of worth is not dependent on what you do, where you come from, or any judgment you may have about yourself. It comes from the very fact of your existence. You are worthy simply because you are!

Meditation for the Heart Chakra

Focus your awareness into your heart. Take a few deep breaths into your chest to release any tightness or constriction you may feel in your rib cage and your back.

The Heart Chakra sits slightly to the right of the center, balancing the physical heart which sits to the left. The colors for the Heart Chakra are green and pink and the form is a pink heart inside a green crescent moon. This acts as a protector to the delicate and pure energy of the heart. It expands across the front and back of the chest, going from shoulder blade to shoulder blade.

- Imagine this green crescent moon stretching across your chest and back. The color of the light radiating from within this crescent is pink. Its properties are: purity; innocence; love; harmony; balance; and brotherhood.

- This light fills your lungs and heart, sending soothing energy down through your arms and out from your hands and fingers. It releases tension in the upper back, behind the shoulder blades, in the elbows, wrists, and fingers. It opens and expands your chest.

- Take a few deep breaths and release any tension in your chest cavity. Concentrate your awareness inside your heart, into the very center of your being.

- Centering in the heart will put you closely in touch with your feelings and calls on your gentleness and tenderness. You may experience a deep quality of love.

- When you listen to your heart you can find answers to questions. By tuning into your heart you may feel sadness or separation, loss or longing. Cherish your feelings and give them space to be there in your heart. You may feel like a pause for some deep breaths or even to release any pent-up feelings with tears. If there is a need to forgive someone who has hurt you then free them from your resentment by forgiving them and let them go. Now forgive yourself. When you listen to your heart you will know what is appropriate.

- Imagine this large green crescent moon radiating soft pink light throughout your upper chest. The more you can let this gentle, pink light into your lungs, chest, upper arms, and back, the freer you become to expand your heart. You are free to love more and more.

- Repeat to yourself:
  "The more love I open myself to receive, the more love I have to give."
  "Love is the purpose of my life."

- Imagine that the light from this green crescent moon is filling your lungs and chest. When you have absorbed enough light then visualize this light pouring out of your chest and back and reaching down towards the solar plexus to embrace the yellow light below it.

  Your heart is now connected to the three lower chakras. You feel a sense of connection and deep tranquillity. You are balanced, in harmony and at peace.

Solar Plexus Affirmations
- I love & accept myself
- I express myself in a powerful way
- I honor myself
- I am authentic
- I am at peace with myself.

Heart Chakra
- I am open to love
- I nurture my inner child
- I forgive myself
- I am peaceful
- I am grateful to all the challenges that helped me to transform & open up to love.

Meditation for the Throat Chakra

Focus your awareness inside your throat. The color for the Throat Chakra is turquoise. The form is an inverted pyramid with the tip pointing towards the heart. The base of this turquoise pyramid is suspended from the jaw and chin.

- Visualize turquoise light pulsing and glowing in your throat and filling your mouth. It strengthens your teeth, tongue, tonsils, and the delicate glands in your throat and neck. It releases tension in your neck, upper back, scalp, jaw, and mouth. The large vertebrae of the atlas and axis are also infused with the light of this chakra.

- The attributes of the Throat Chakra are: creativity; self-expression; spiritual will; and clear communication.

    As you breathe into this center it becomes vitalized and these properties expand and increase in scope daily.

- Take several deep breaths and release any tension which you are holding in your throat or jaw. You may find that your throat feels tight or constricted. There may be compression in the back of your neck. Perhaps you suffer from headaches which affect your neck and occipital region. Take three deep, relaxing breaths and release your tongue to fall into the back of your throat.

- Gently let the lower jaw drop forward to release any tension. Focus your awareness in your throat where energy can so easily slip away or be dissipated.

- Visualize this turquoise pyramid suspended from your jaw, radiating light into the bones of your skull and upper spine. Let the light illuminate the intricate and delicate formation of your vocal apparatus. Bring the light into your mouth, into the gums and the living roots of your teeth. As the light shines into your mouth release the tension from your hard palate. As you visualize this color energizing and soothing tension in your neck and throat, imagine that bacteria and catarrh are dissolving and you are left with a clean throat and mouth.

- Repeat to yourself:
  "I allow the expression of my true self to find form."
  "I express myself creatively and openly."
  "I can harness my will for my creative and spiritual development."

- Let the line shine from your throat and embrace the light in your Heart Chakra. All the chakras blend into one harmonious unit of colors. All this continued feeling of expansion and connectedness to move along your spine. Your throat opens and you feel deeply connected to the feelings in your heart and the thoughts in your mind.

Meditation for the Brow Chakra

The Brow Chakra is located between your eyes at the point where your nose joins your forehead. Focus your awareness in this space. Begin to take several deep, releasing breaths. This will slowly free any tension which you may be holding in your head.

The color of the Brow Chakra is indigo blue. The form is a large star whose points of light radiate throughout your head.

- Imagine this star beaming a brilliant indigo light throughout your entire skull. The light penetrates your skull and brain deep into the brain stem. It permeates and enlivens all your senses. Your sight, hearing, smell, and taste are heightened. This indigo star penetrates deep into your awareness, giving you a feeling of stillness, and tranquillity.

- As this indigo star radiates energy into your head you feel clear and detached from anything which would engage your energy. You are clam and centered within yourself. As you release the tension in and around your head you begin to enjoy the cool, soothing energy of the indigo star working to heal and restore your tranquillity.

- The qualities of the indigo star are: concentration; clarity; detachment; intelligence; and awareness.

  As you do this meditation these qualities are expanding and developing within you.

- Take several deep breaths and release the tension you are holding behind your eyes and in your skull cavity. Your scalp is actually becoming looser as you imagine your head bathed in this cool indigo light.

Repeat to yourself:
"I radiate love, clarity, and integrity."
"My thoughts are clear and focused."
"I know who I am."
"My purpose in light is becoming clear to me."

- Visualize this indigo star beaming light into every cell of your brain. When you have absorbed all the light that you need for yourself begin to radiate light out through your brow and from the back of your head. Let this light encompass and embrace the turquoise light from your Throat Chakra. Now you are connected to all your other chakras. You feel expanded, stimulated, and tranquil. All is well in your life. You are at peace with yourself. You are in control of your future through your clear and positive thoughts.

Meditation for the Crown Chakra

Bring your awareness to the top of your head, the area of the Crown Chakra. Its color is violet, its form is a skull cap that gently over the chakra.

- Imagine rays of violet light from your crown spreading down over your head covering your whole body with a soft, beautiful glow of energy. Visualize a cloak of light which protects you and seals in your energy. It is soothing and healing. It gives you a feeling of tranquillity, deep peace, and protection.

- The attributes of the Crown Chakra are: cosmic consciousness; unity; communion; inner peace; refinement; beauty; and grace. As you meditate on these qualities they grow and expand within you. You became these qualities.

- Breathe into the top of your head and free the Crown Chakra to open easily as you receive the vibrations of higher inspiration.

- Take in the feelings of beauty and goodness, light and purity. Allow yourself to feel enveloped in this cloak of protection and grace. You are at one with the Universal Intelligence. You have connected to a deep sense of peace within yourself. You feel at one with yourself and with life.

- As you sit under this violet skull cap you are safe and at rest. Your wounds are being healed. You trust in the Source of life. There is silence, tranquillity, freedom and beauty as you absorb this violet light into your entire body. When you have taken what you need for yourself, imagine a radiant beam of violet light shining down from the very top of your head. This light envelops you and all the other chakras. You are connected, expanded, whole and complete.

- Repeat to yourself:
  "I am at one with the universe."
  "I am at peace."

Dowsing the Chakras

Dowsing is a very useful way to measure the energetic flow of electromagnetic energy circulating around the chakras. This energy flow is a direct reflection of the quality of positive or negative thoughts we have about the specific emotional issues contained within each chakra. I use the pendulum to assess the degree of flow and to ascertain the quality of energy.

Although emotional energy is very subtle in nature it can also be gauged through body language and vocal resonance. Tension, which is released at a physical level, is also released emotionally and energetically throughout our entire systems. The degree of imploded or blocked energy, or the degree of its freedom of flow, can be measured with the pendulum.

The pendulum also demonstrates how energy shifts when you have positive or affirmative thoughts. Negativity can actually reverse the course of a pendulum from its natural flow, putting it into a negative spin. The following section will help you to use the pendulum as a diagnostic tool in healing work. It will also give you visible evidence of energy moving through the chakra system.

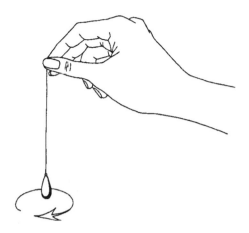

1   *Making a Pendulum*

Find something which will serve as a pendulum. I have used lead fishing weights, shower curtain rings, crystals, and even car keys and tea bags. Anything that can swing freely will suffice.

2   *Practice Swinging the Pendulum*

Hold the pendulum steady in your right hand. Suspending it from a short string will allow the pendulum to rotate easily.

Practice swinging it around so you can feel what it is like when you move it intentionally. This feels different from when it begins to move in response to the electro-magnetic energy flowing through you.

3   *Find the Still Point within Yourself*

Find the still point within yourself. You may want to sit quietly for a few moments. Holding the pendulum in your right hand, swing it about 2–3 inches over the open palm of your left hand. There are chakras in both your hands. The pendulum will begin to move in response to the energy field coming off your hand. Be still and wait quietly for this to happen. Be willing to let go of any skeptical or negative thoughts about this so that it can happen for you.

4 Which Direction Is Positive and Which Is Negative?

Ask your Higher Self to show you which direction is positive and which is negative for you. Hold the pendulum steady and watch which way it is moving. If you are open to this form of receiving information then there will probably not be any resistance to the pendulum moving. If, however, you are skeptical and fearful of receiving information from your Higher Self in this form it may take you a while to have visible evidence that the pendulum can work for you. If it is slow, be patient.

5 Placing the Pendulum Over a Chakra

Hold the pendulum over a friend's chakra or one of your own. Hold the pendulum 3 inches from the chakra. The pendulum should start to move. This is a measure of your magnetic energy. If you are doing this to someone it will reflect both you and your partner's energy.

6 Feeling the Degree of Movement and the Positive or Negative Polarity

Hold the pendulum steady and get a feeling for the degree of movement, its velocity, and the smoothness or ease with which it swings around.

Ask your Higher Self which direction is positive and which is negative, and notice the degree of intensity with which it moves in that direction. For instance, if it is turning in a negative direction, is it swinging quickly or is it barely turning in that pole?

7 How Your Thoughts Influence the Flow of Your Energy

Visualize a color which relates to the chakra you are working on. It may be red for the Root, orange for the Sacral, yellow for the Solar Plexus, green or pink for the Heart, turquoise for the Throat, indigo blue for the Brow, or violet for the Crown.

Use your imagination to intensify the color in your mind's eye. Watch the pendulum as you are doing this visualization. It may start to move faster or the circle may grow as you do this visualization.

You have now established a strong flow of energy with the pendulum. Now remember a very negative experience from your past.

It may be a time when you were very sad, humiliated, or grief-stricken. It may be a current situation which you are having a problem trying to resolve.

Watch the pendulum move. It may reverse direction, moving with negative polarity. This is a direct result of your negative thoughts and feelings.

You can change this movement to a positive polarity by simply thinking very positive thoughts or remembering a time when you were very happy and contented. Watch the pendulum start to move again in a positive direction. This is the power of thought which can change and transform energy. I think it is also evidence of our ability to transform our own reality with positive thinking. It also demonstrates how strongly negative thinking can affect us. Remember: "Energy follows thought."

8 Getting a Chakra Reading

To get a reading of a chakra hold the pendulum in the area of the chakra. Hold the pendulum about 2–3 inches in front of the chakra. If you are intent on getting a reading you can actually hold the pendulum anywhere and be shown a measure of that chakra's energy. In the same way you can use the pendulum to obtain information about many different things which you may like to know.

Note the degree of velocity, if there is a torsion to the movement. Sometimes there is an imbalance in the flow of energy and the pendulum may describe an eclipse rather than a circle. Use your sensitivity to ascertain if the movement feels sluggish or hesitant. These qualities and other will become more apparent to you as you get more practice with the pendulum. You may try asking the pendulum itself what certain qualities of movement mean. Obviously it will only respond yes or no, so frame your questions in such a way that you are given a clear answer.

For instance, you may see that there is a pull to the right over a particular chakra. Ask the pendulum: Does this signify uncertainty or confusion about a particular emotional issue? I have used the pendulum to give me answers to family situations about which I had no information. I have met people who have even used it to find the exact time of their birth.

9 *Measuring the Degree to Which You Have Shifted Energy*
When you have finished the chakra massage (for more on this, see the next chapter), dowse again to see the degree of freedom and movement that has taken place in the chakra. You will be surprised to see the shift that has taken place, so clearly indicated by the changed movement of the pendulum before and after the massage.

The Layers of the Chakras
and the Chakra Massage

The Chakra massage is very gentle and non-intrusive. At the same time it has the ability to shift and release tremendous amounts of energy which may be blocking and congesting your energy system. It can be done with clothes either on or off. No oil or powder is required. It is best done using only the friction of your hand. This is an energetic massage. It works on the subtle, etheric body rather than the physical body. It does, however, give a deep sense of relaxation and it can feel wonderfully sensual and pleasurable. It helps restore the natural flow of energy by releasing blocked energy from the chakras.

The Top Layer of the Chakra
Each chakra has three layers of energy. This massage works on the top layer. It gives a great sense of well-being and peace. It can help to re-establish a deep connection to self.

The top layer of energy within each chakra relates to transpersonal energy. This is the energy which can become congested in the comings and goings of everyday life, especially when we forget our spiritual nature and ignore our truest purpose in life. The blockages in this field of energy come about through unexpressed emotions. These blockages reflect our capacity to experience, express, and release our feelings. This form of massage is very effective when it is done to us or we do it to someone. It shifts our focus away from deep wounds to a damaged ego. This massage activates the body's memory of being loved and cared for. We need this energy flow to keep us alive, active, and healthy. While this massage works well to decongest the top layer of the chakra it also nourishes us by soothing and satisfying our natural longing for touch and healing.

The Middle Layer of the Chakra
The second or middle layer of the chakra relates to deeply personal emotional issues. These may require a deeper therapeutic approach to work through the disturbances which focus around our birthing, infancy, and early childhood.

When the chakra is blocked at this level the mind needs to be engaged and committed to reprogramming negative thoughts about the past. Unresolved issues which stand in the way of our development and growth are best worked through cognitively (i.e., through our mental processes) as well as energetically. I would recommend workshops or private sessions with a healer, psychotherapist, or rebirther.

The Deep Inner Core of the Chakra
The deep core of the chakra is related to the soul path. To disturb the patterns which are locked into the energetic code would be a violation of a person's life process. No one can know the deep unfolding of the soul's destiny. However, these very deep layers of energy are more likely to open and blossom when the top layers are free from congestion.

Beginning the Massage: Creating a Comfortable Space
Create a warm, comfortable space in which to do this massage. You can use a massage table or a firm, comfortable surface such as a bed, or you can work on a mat on the floor.

I always have a candle burning and I enjoy working next to an open fire. I light incense to purify the air in the room. I also have soothing music playing and have several crystals around to absorb and neutralize the energy which is being released. A beautiful environment helps to soothe and relax both you and the person you are working with.

Where To Begin
The massage begins at the Root Chakra. For this chakra you and your partner will need to be on his or her front. Ask your partner to lie on his or her stomach, face down. For all the other chakras you will be working on both the front and the back of your partner. The front is where we "pull" congested energy from the chakra. The back of the body is where we massage the surface of the body, as it is less threatening and intrusive. We are much more vulnerable when we expose the soft, tender front of the body.

Pulling Out Congested Energy
The first step to massaging the chakras is to "pull" congested energy out of the chakra. (See the diagram on next page.) This is done by slowly drawing a circle with the tips of your fingers clockwise around the Root Chakra. As your fingers swirl around, start to lift energy which is imploded and congested in the chakra as if you were lifting candy floss. Pull the energy up and out of the chakra with your fingertips. Then throw it away. Have a candle burning while you do this exercise and throw the energy into the fire, which is purifying and will burn the energetic dross.

The Massage
The next step is to massage the chakra (See the diagram on page 38). Do this with the palm of the right hand. The right hand is the giving hand.

It feeds energy into the chakra allowing energy to be released. Using the right hand also prevents you from taking the excess dross into your own energetic system.

With your right hand gently rub across the area of the chakra for approximately ten minutes. Anchor your left hand on the body to keep the energetic polarity flowing.

You may wish to use soft, soothing music while you work, or to hum, sing or chant to your partner. Sound opens channels for healing to occur

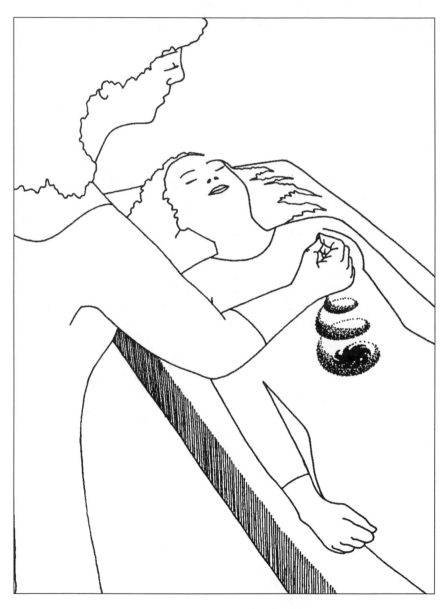

"Pulling" congested energy out of the chakra. (See page 35.)

and there is nothing which can soothe and comfort like the richness of the human voice.

As you start to rub gently across the chakra with your right hand try to develop a sense that your partner is responding to your touch. You could either make figures of eight, rub back and forth, or make circles with your hand. The essential thing is not to break the energetic contact with your partner.

Ask your partner to take some deep connecting breaths. As you do this massage there will be moments when the energy will feel stuck and congested. This is when it is appropriate to use deep breathing to assist you in freeing the energy. We connect to our life-force through our breath. It helps to clear the imploded energy which accumulates in the chakra.

Use the left hand to rock the body gently back and forth. This will help your partner to unwind and free up tension.

As you move up to the higher centers the energy becomes more refined. It is important to be very aware and gentle as you begin to move up into the higher realms of energy.

In the lower chakras it is appropriate to be firm and more assertive as you do the massage, but as you approach the heart and face it is important to realize you are working where a person is most sensitive.

Note:
There is one very important point regarding working with the Heart Chakra. Never work directly on the heart. Please look at the detailed instructions in he chapter for the Heart Chakra. A specific indirect movement is used over the heart area.

Rhythm and Tempo of the Massage
You may wish to change the tempo or rhythm of the movements you are using in this massage to suit the energy of your partner. At times it may feel appropriate to go faster or slower, to use a firmer or a lighter touch. When you keep the touch light, your partner will be able to bring his or her awareness up into your hands and help you to release their congested energy. You may also ask the person what kind of touch they

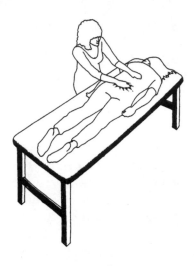

Massage the chakra.

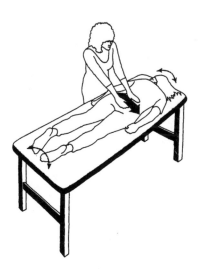

Decongest blocked energy by gently rocking the body back and forth.

enjoy. A firm touch may be appreciated, particularly in the lower chakras. For the person experiencing the massage there may be sensations of warmth flooding into the area you working on. This is a sign that energy is shifting, being released, and beginning to open.

Feeling the Emotions as They Rise to Consciousness

As you begin to decongest the chakra, strong emotions may flood the conscious mind. If there has been emotional suppression you may feel anger, frustration, sadness or grief. Allow these feelings to arise in you and be willing to experience the power of your own feelings. At the same time that energy gets released, there may also be visual and auditory phenomena. Tingling in the hands, feet, and mouth may occur. This happens when energy is being released and does not last for very long. If it should occur, breathe deeply and regularly and let the energy release.

Support your partner by encouraging them to feel whatever comes up for them. Help them to breathe through their feelings. Be sure they do not hyperventilate; consistent, gentle breaths allow the feelings to emerge and be experienced. Hyperventilation will charge the body too strongly and take you out of your experience. Your partner may need to cry in order to express his or her feelings. Be there for them so they experience support and can trust themselves to open to their own inner feelings.

Using Affirmations During The Massage

Your partner may find it useful to say an affirmation repeatedly to themselves while you work to unblock and release their energy. There are several affirmations which relate to each chakra in the appropriate chapter.

When you have finished the massage a large amount of blocked emotional energy will have been released. It is essential to remember that we are only facilitators in allowing this emotional energy to be released. We should never try to force or demand more to be released than is ready to come out at any point. Whatever a person is prepared to experience is enough for their shift in consciousness at that moment. The more we can stay out of the way and let this release happen, the better it is for the person experiencing it.

Sealing the Chakras

Sealing the chakras is a way of encapsulating the energy of the chakras in light. It restores balance and harmony to your energy system and prevent energy from escaping out of the chakra after you have cleansed it. This technique protects the whole energetic field. I use a candle in a small dish to seal the chakra in light. You could just as well use a torch or visualize light coming out of your hands and moving around the body.

This exercise is very relaxing and soothing. I learned it from Monica Antony, a healer working in London. It gives strength and balance to the subtle bodies within the auric field.

Take a candle and trace an outline of a cross of light within a circle of light three times around the body (see the diagram on page 28). Always move in a clockwise direction.

After you have drawn a circle around the body make individual crosses of light within circles of light around each chakra. Again move in a clockwise direction.

When you have completed making a cross of light within a circle of light around the chakra, circle the body three times, again moving clockwise.

Make a cross of light within a circle of light across the entire body. Make the cross from the top of the head to the base of the spine, and then across the chest at the point where the arms join the trunk.

Do this on the back and then on the front of the body when you have finished the massage. You can do this after working on all the chakras or on one particular chakra. It is a form of energetic cleansing, burning the cross that has accumulated in the massage work. It seals and protects the delicate energy of the chakra and strengthens the auric field.

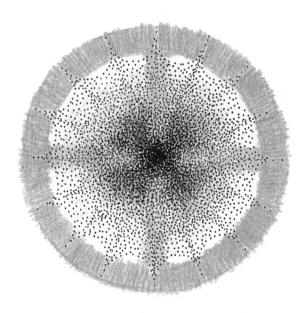

The cross of light within a circle of light, used for sealing the chakras.

Summary of Part One

Working with the Chakras

The following are the techniques I use in working with the chakras.

1 *Movement and breathing*

Move to any music which inspires you to move freely. Let yourself move, releasing tension, opening and stretching your body. Activate your breathing and release any stale air from your lungs. Use the "release" breath as often as you need to let go of congested energy.

2 *Meditation*

Sit comfortably with your spine straight or lie on your back, knees up in a semi-supine position. Place a 3-inch book under your head. Visualize the colors and forms of each chakra. Become centered, tranquil, and peaceful and you reflect on the chakras, their colors and shapes.

3 *Dowsing*

Use a pendulum to ascertain the flow of energy in each chakra before and after massage. This is a way to measure negative and positive energy.

4 *Massage*

Follow the instructions for decongesting and massaging the chakras. Create balance and harmony in your energetic system.

5 *Seal the chakras*

Seal the chakras with a cross of light within a circle of light. Seal the auric field as well.

Now that we have looked at the various techniques for working with subtle energy, we will go on in Part Two to explore each of the seven main chakras in detail. You may find it useful to make notes as a record of your progress and there are some pages available at the end of the book for this purpose.

Part Two
The Chakras

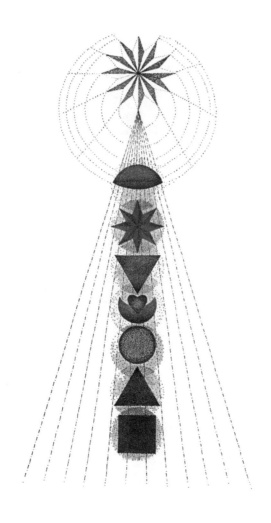

The Root Chakra

Element: Earth

Archetype: The Mother

Sense: smell

Shape: a cube

Sound: "La" (to be chanted into the Root Chakra)

Soul lesson: service

The Root Chakra is located at the base of the spine in the perineum. In ancient texts it is symbolically represented as a square or cube. The Egyptians called it "the field" because it looked like a cross-section of land and, coincidentally, the element which governs this chakra is Earth. It is ruled by the nourishing aspect of the Mother archetype. Its primary function is to root the spirit securely in the physical reality of human existence.

Genetic Inheritance

This chakra is the center which governs the basic earthly instincts needed for physical survival. These ensure that we have sufficient food and shelter, as well as the means whereby they can be consistently obtained. Success and failure in our physical survival become embodied in the Root Chakra and are handed down from generation to generation. Central to our physical continuance on this planet are the requirements for good health, and continuation of the species. These functions are programmed into our genetic material. Our continued nourishment and survival are related to how deeply we tap into our roots. The etheric template for our physical development and evolution lies within our genetic code. This means that the potential for all we can become is locked within our genes. We have within our consciousness the ability to transform patterns of survival which no longer serve us in civilized societies, such as attitudes of dominance, violence, and war-mongering. We can shift energy which has been used for basic survival and transmute it into higher consciousness for our joy, well-being, and creativity.

People who lack the curiosity to explore the full potential of their lives energetically tend to be strongly guilt-ridden, depressed, and conditioned by parental example. Such people may be willing subconsciously to cooperate with and attract disease, accident, and violence.

Depending on how past generations of your family saw life, whether as a struggle or as a worthwhile experience to be lived and enjoyed, this in turn will determine the unconscious patterns you carry in your Root Chakra.

If your family was positive, affirmative, and felt supported by life, you will probably carry a similar attitude (within your roots) and find life generally easy. The template for your life's potential creativity will be strong and vital. You will be able to adapt to stress and change. For those who do not have this early positive programming, it becomes essential for your well-being consciously to create this model for ease, trust, and good health.

If your family constantly struggled for survival, you may well carry many negative qualities such as suspicion, cunning, greed, and insecurity through to situations where you feel your own survival to be threatened. This may be reflected in your attitude to money, posses-sions, and relationships. Any long-term prospect of believing in an abundant universe will probably be difficult for you until these innately pessimistic attitudes are healed.

Group Survival Instinct

The Root Chakra also influences tribal or clan attitudes. Familial and ethnic group instincts for survival are all reflected in the Root Chakra. The attitudes which any particular group embrace and embody for col-lective life maintenance will have been programmed into you. They will influence the flow of energy from your Root Chakra towards the earth, and block the rise of energy into higher realms of individuation and spiritual experience.

If your family, clan, or tribe needed to draw on your energy simply in order to help them survive, then you may well have a hard time find-ing your own individuality. When and if you do decide to pull away from your collective roots there will be many things which may appear to hold back your development. Calls of family duty, job responsibilities, or financial obligations will loom large in your consciousness. You may feel that you cannot do the things you desire most and which would ful-fill your individual creativity. Every time something happens to your clan or collective group you will experience it in your body.

A very striking example of this survival instinct happened at the beginning of the Gulf War when Saddam Hussein threatened to annihi-late Israel. That very same Sunday morning the local Jewish delicatessens in Manchester enjoyed a sudden and unprecedented rush which cleared them out of bagels. Now if you were to ask those Jewish people who were caught up in that rather bizarre great bagel rush why they were there I am sure they would have difficulty giving you a rational explanation. This collective gesture of solidarity was born out of a profoundly instinctive "root" reaction to their racial survival under threat.

Basic Attitudes

When the Root Chakra is open and functional it will support us in manifesting all of our creative desires. It is in direct proportion to how

46

grounded we are on the physical plane that we are able to realize our dreams.

The basic attitudes we have which support our life-force, both individually and collectively, are reflected in the quality of energy in the Root Chakra. If you or people in your family or clan have been denied ease, comfort, or reasonably good health, then life may appear to be difficult and unfair. These attitudes may well show up in the relationships you pick, your job choices, how you feel towards education and gaining freedom to advance both socially and economically. It will color how you see the opposite sex. It may show up in your attitudes to what you feel you deserve, and what demands you will permit yourself to make of the world. These fixed attitudes will either block or activate the energy in your Root Chakra.

It is when you are stressed or ill that the most basic unconscious attitudes about life appear. They may manifest as despair, defeat, indifference, or lack of confidence. Most of us identify with these ideas about ourselves and our lives without ever detaching ourselves and making the space to observe our chronic patterns. Your ideas may be narrow-minded or bigoted, depending on how much you feel others rightly deserve, or how much you feel you can take for yourself. They may appear as atavistic, racial, or class attitudes, tribal in origin, which are hostile and excluding to "outsiders." They will most certainly have been sparked off by fear. Fear is the single greatest limitation to experiencing life that there is. For instance, if your great-grandfather was a miner struggling against cold, damp, and poverty, trying to support a large family, he might have had strong political views or a spiritual outlook that did not embrace ease, comfort, or abundance.

These attitudes will have been passed down with each generation, no matter how well they did economically or how well educated they became in later years. And so that is how you may now have the idea that life is a bitter struggle and that there is much to fear. And thus even the root of this attitude may be four generations old and your present reality quite different. Repeated patterns become imprinted in our genetic code. Ideas get passed down from generation to generation. All old negative attitudes become anchored in the fight-or-flight function of the adrenal cortex of our kidneys. These are the ductless glands which process the energy from the Root Chakra as hormonal secretions flowing into the bloodstream.

Our primal attitudes about "how life is" are thus rooted in our physical bodies. They also show themselves in body armoring and posture. We are always revealing our received truths, fears, and attitudes simply through our body language. The body is a perfect metaphor for our internal reality and we can even learn to read this language if we wish. Health and healing are created by internal shifts of perception. The attitudes we are born with reflect what we feel we deserve from life and they intrinsically confirm what we will give back to the life-force by way of our creative output.

The positive qualities of the Root Chakra are stability, structure, security, and manifestation. A sense of time, order, constancy, and commitment are also part of the groundedness which make up the nature of this energy. These form our link to harmony and the path through which we grow and develop easily. Stability and order enhance creativity. Without these qualities there would be constant chaos and disruption. Though we would survive we would be confronting fear as a constant disruptive element. This would stop us from concentrating on our growth, development, and creative expression. People who constantly experience fear or restlessness may want to examine the nature of their roots. Within them lie vital clues as to why their Root Chakra is congested, blocking the flow of their emotional energy.

Grounding

In Bioenergetic Therapy the function of the Root Chakra is called "grounding." This literally means having a strong physical and emotional foundation. Grounding entails focusing on and responsibly tackling the details of everyday life. It implies practicality and a realistic approach to problems. People who are grounded are fundamentally sound and make good judgments based on true instincts and clear thinking. In turn, good grounding helps us reach higher levels of awareness, understanding and, ultimately, joy. This process creates a strong energetic foundation on which to develop our full potential.

The energy flowing from the Root Chakra directly influences the hormonal output of the adrenal cortex. This root energy flows to the skeletal system, the circulatory system, and to the legs and feet, the parts of the body which support our physical existence and give us our grounding in the physical world. If you have a problem with issues of grounding which may show up as restlessness or anxiety about personal safety, you may be experiencing a dysfunctional Root Chakra. It can also manifest in chronic lower back pain, sciatica, varicose veins, rectal maladies, or poor circulation to the legs and feet. Our attitudes to safety and security will also reflect how well we are rooted in ourselves. These attitudes are often unconscious and may relate to how we were birthed. Remarkably, the attitudes of our parents at the time of our conception also have been known to influence our perspective on life. Tribal or racial attitudes which our parents carried from their forebears and which were transmitted to us through gestation, birthing, or early childhood rearing also affect the energy in the Root Chakra. They will directly affect the degree of function or dysfunction of this basic life-force of energy which we need for physical survival and creative manifestation. The ways in which they may affect you would very from degrees of frustration or restlessness at times of stress, to overblown violence and rage as a reaction to deep-rooted fear and insecurity about life.

Financial insecurity and anxiety about being able to provide fundamental care for yourself or your family will also tend to congest the Root Chakra. When energy becomes congested in the Root Chakra the basic underlying themes of fear and anxiety block the connection to your life energy. This block will then impede the grounding of vital life energy and this ungroundedness will reflect the views about life which have been passed down through the generations of your family who struggled with survival. Often Past Life Regression can reveal the themes of these struggles. It is significant that people with terminal illness always have depleted Root Chakra energy. Their soul pulls their energy up from the physical into the higher centers of spiritual awareness for their journey home.

With consciousness-raising work, energy becomes free in the chakras and goes back into feeding your life-force. This energy can be used for your good health, well-being, pleasure, and creativity.

An example of this is well illustrated in the case of a young man whose father came to England from an Eastern Bloc country after the Second World War. This man married an English woman and had several children. Though he was able to work and provide for his family he was very restless. In turn his son was also unable to settle in any one place, job, or relationship. He carried the negative energy of his father's dislocation within his Root Chakra. However, by examining these patterns of unrootedness in his life and his father's life, he was able to transform this blocked energy. He was also able to confront his own fears and anxieties through the straightforward process of understanding his own roots. Through energetic work on a body level he could make these patterns conscious. And what is crucial to notice is that he not only healed himself through this process but his father also got great benefit as well. The energy in his Root Chakra became open and he is now far more stable and grounded within himself.

Try to imagine a fully grown tree becoming uprooted. If you brought it to a new location to be replanted you would need to re-establish all the same conditions which were optimal for its earlier growth. You would want to have the same or similar climate, the same type of soil, and so on. There would be so many factors necessary for recreating the conditions for growth and continued life. People who have been uprooted from their natural home have to go through a similar re-orientation. Even if they left their native soil because they couldn't survive there they still carry the imprint of that "home" with them wherever they go. They must find a good place to put down their roots or find these safe roots deep within themselves.

If you were to look at the distribution of different ethnic groups in the United States, for instance, it is apparent that most peoples established themselves in places similar to their homeland. The Spanish went to California, which is hot, dry, and resembles Spain. The Swedes went to the northern regions where they found harsh, cold-weather conditions. The Germans went to the middle of America and were followed by cultures which found climates similar to those they had left behind. New England is very like England, and the southern states where Black people were brought over as slaves have a similarity to Africa in climate and soil. Otherwise, given the harshness and difficulty of their conditions, they most probably could not have survived. These cultures all took root in America in areas where they felt they could survive.

Healing Our Roots

In homeopathy the patterns of the roots of disease are being investigated by Dr. Rajan Shankaran. He feels we carry the roots of family or tribal delusions in our cells and that these can cause disease when activated by stress. Shankaran says when a delusion or attitude persists for long periods of time, then the pattern becomes fixed and encoded within our genetic material. This, in turn, becomes a dysfunctional root which when stimulated by stress or external irritation will flare into a disease pattern.

At source we are all channels of energy which offer radiant and unlimited potential for creativity. All that blocks this flow are our fixed ideas about ourselves and how we feel life should be. Many of these attitudes are unconscious and come as part of our inheritance. We are an amalgam of all the attitudes which came before our actual birth as well as those we form ourselves.

Individuation is learning to separate ourselves from collective patterns which block our life-force. One of the ways we can do this is by examining the root attitudes we carry. These patterns are woven deeply into the subconscious structure of the mind and are reflected in the energetic system. By examining our roots we make ourselves conscious of these attitudes. We become conscious masters of our lives rather than helpless victims or martyrs.

James Hillman speaks about the abandoned child within our psyche in his book *Loose Ends*. He says this child never leaves us. What we can learn to do is let this child guide and direct our inner life rather than punish or correct this child as he or she was punished in youth. Similarly, if those patterns which have to do with the quality of our survival on this planet become conscious, they too can direct and guide us to the kind of lifestyle we would desire for ourselves. What we need to do is to be willing to look at those patterns which we carry, and create positive affirmations which will help to open and direct our energy. This is the first step towards healing our roots.

The individual ego is not separate from the collective ego of the tribe or clan. This is how groups survived difficult times. Individual desires, urges, and needs for expression were all subordinated to the common good. What this means at a personal level is that one's life-force was used to support the collective life-force. This occurs at a family level when one's individuality and creativity is suppressed to feed a family myth. It may take therapy to start to unravel the depths of who we individually are.

The positive side of this group spirit is that everyone gets looked after. No one is excluded because of what they are within the context of the group. The negative aspect is that the individual can't easily grow and express himself. In order to individuate, to break away from the collective dictates of the tribe, people have had to pull away and leave the comfort and security of their families and clans. This creates fear and insecurity. When we face these monsters, as they are often depicted in fairy tales and myths, then we grow, mature, and find inner strength.

Movements for the Root Chakra
The rhythms for the base chakra are loud and rhythmical, like Afro-Cuban sounds. They inspire us to get up and dance and were created to move people and uplift the spirit.

Any strongly rhythmical music which will inspire you to move is perfectly suitable for this experience. Doing movement to music is pleasurable and enjoyable and takes away any sense of exercising. Let these movements be fun and joyful for you.

The movements for the Root Chakra involve the feet, legs, and hips. They are repetitious and highly charged with energy. They will ground you to earth in a unique way which allows energy to flow through you. The more you move the more energy you will generate.

1 Stand with your feet about shoulder-width apart. Start by twisting your torso from side to side, letting the arms swing freely. This loosens the spine and takes tension out of the neck and shoulders. Release your jaw and breathe out through your mouth as you twist your body back and forth.

2 Bend your knees and begin to swing your pelvis from front to back. Release your bum so you are not holding in the tight muscles of the buttocks and hamstring muscles. With your hand on your hips, cock your hips backwards. Take in a breath as you do so. As you thrust your pelvis forward, release your breath out. You may wish to make noises as you do so. This will free up even more energy. Repeat this movement several times until you feel connected in your movement and with your breath. Keep the knees loose and flexible.

3 Spread your feet further apart. Begin by lifting the arms to your side and releasing the spine down towards the floor as you let your knees give way into a bend. This is actually releasing the Root Chakra down towards the earth. The movement is repeated as you raise yourself by straightening your knees.

4 With your feet in a wide stance and your knees bent and turned outward let your pelvis move back and forward in a wide, circular, swinging movement.

5 Another movement that is excellent for opening the Root Chakra is as follows. Spread your feet about a foot apart. Now rise up on to your toes and then, bending the knees, slam the heels down into the ground. Repeat this several times. Emphasis is on the downward movements of the heels. As you go down on the heels release your breath and let out a sound.

6 Walk on your toes with your arms raised in the air. Shake your hips from side to side. This is opening and freeing, no inhibition allowed.

Gabrielle Roth, a modern American shaman, dancer, and teacher, told me many years ago, "Your soul is on the bottoms of your feet."

Massage for the Root Chakra

The location for the Root Chakra is at the very base of the spine. To do the Root Chakra massage, make sure your partner is comfortable lying on their stomach, face down. Be sure they are warm—doing this massage can make body temperature drop.

Because this is an energetic massage it works equally well if you are dressed or naked. If you do it without clothing you won't need oil or powder. The simple friction of your hand will work sufficiently well.

1 Begin by placing your right hand over the base of the spine. Anchor your left hand on the body to maintain the energy polarity.

2 Begin by drawing the blocked energy out of the body by making clockwise circles with your hands and pulling the energy out of the chakra. Flick the excess energy away from you, preferably directing it towards a candle or bowl of water.

3 Next, begin to massage the Root Chakra by gently rubbing back and forth across the hip joints with your right hand.

4 You can make figures of eight, clockwise circles or continue to rub back and forth with your right hand. Your partner may wish to have stronger or lighter pressure, or faster or slower movements. Be sure to ask what they prefer.

5 If your partner becomes uncomfortable because of awakening sensations, encourage them to breathe through the discomfort. Stay connected, stay tranquil, and give your partner the opportunity to experience whatever is occurring for them.

6 Do this massage for 10–20 minutes.

Color of the Root Chakra

The color of the Root Chakra is red. This indicates force, vigor, and vitality. It is the color of warmth, love, and passion. Treating disease with this color stimulates the autonomic nervous system and the circulatory system. If over-used it can create irritation and excitement. A dark, cloudy red in the aura indicates a high temper and nervous turmoil. A light, thin red suggests a nervous, impulsive, and self-centered person with few reserves of energy. A coarse shade of red reveals a tyrannic or despotic nature. It suggests a ruthless nature which will do anything to achieve what it wants. Red emphasized in the aura suggests that this person would make a good soldier or adventurer—they will thrive on action. People with a lot of red in their aura are earthy, lusty, passionate people. They often have difficulty relaxing or concentrating.

Red is the color which is first noticed by visual perception. Red light can raise the pulse rate. It is used to warm and stimulate the system. When used in healing it is contraindicated for hardening of the arteries, varicose veins or ulcerated or infected veins, history of heart trouble, high blood pressure, clots or thrombosis, strokes or hemorrhages. Use red to stimulate, to bring up deeply congested life energy, and to earth a person.

Healing Uses for the Color Red

It stimulates the circulation, building hemoglobin. It feeds the senses and is of benefit when there is a lack of sensory stimulation. It nourishes the liver, giving it energy and tone.

It is also good for:
Depression
Anemia
Frostbite
Neuralgia
Paralysis
Aches and pains in the lower back, buttocks, legs and feet
Infertility

Attributes of the Root Chakra

Positive	*Negative*
Life-force	Violence
Survival	Fear
Stability	Frustration
Security	Restlessness
Manifestation	Rootlessness
Patience	Alienation
Commitment	Separation
Constancy	Dishonesty
Will	Cunning
Passion	
Sexuality	
Ambition	

Gemstones
Garnet
Ruby
Tourmaline
Smoky Quartz
Bloodstone
Black Onyx
Quartz

Aromas
The following oils are generally grounding and tonifying:

Cedarwood
Musk compounds
Veti Vert—gives protection and
    balance
Cypress oil
Civet
Patchouli—grounds mental energy
Myrrh—energizes
Frankincense—resonates with the Crown Chakra
Rosewood
Elemi—unites the body and the spirit
Garlic
Clove

To find out more about the effects of Aromatherapy on the chakras I would recommend reading Patricia Davis's *Subtle Aromatherapy* (C.W. Daniel).

Questionnaire for the Root Chakra

1 How strongly do you feel that you belong (to yourself, your family, tribe, clan or race, nation)?

2 Do you feel a sense of responsibility to defend your family, tribe, nation or race?

3 Do you feel that you can stand on your own feet and survive in the world?

4 Do you recognize who and what supports you?

5 Do you feel you can provide the necessities of life for yourself and your family?

6 Do you come from a family background where issues of poverty, extreme religious affiliation, class, or financial insecurity were part of your childhood? How have those conditions affected your view of life?

7 What are your fears, insecurities, anxieties?

8 If something happened to your "lifelines" (your means of survival), could you look after yourself?

9 Do your family and friends support you in achieving your independence, growth, and creativity?

10 Who do you feel is ultimately responsible for your life?

11 Look at your response to these questions. Evaluate what holds you back from developing. Who and what *supports* your growth and development?

12 Can you see more autonomy entering your life?

Affirmations for the Root Chakra

I am safe and secure at all times.

I am divinely protected and guided and my way is made smooth and easy.

I love my feet. They show me the way.

I love my legs. They give me support.

I am open to expanding my awareness of life.

I am willing to release all my old patterns of fear and insecurity to live with joy and well-being. Now!

I know that I belong. I know that I am safe.

People now support me in an easy and pleasurable way.

It is safe for me to enjoy my life now.

I am willing to be my own good mother and look after myself properly at all times.

I am responsible for the quality of my life.

I am open to new ideas, new thoughts, and new people in my life.

I am willing to consider the possibility that there are new approaches to enjoying life which will enhance my sense of being alive and give me pleasure.

Life is good.

I trust life will support me in fulfilling my purpose.

I have a right to be me, just exactly as I am.

I have a right to express myself and manifest my dreams.

I can have pleasure without painful consequences.

Nobody wants to hurt me.

I trust in the process of my life to unfold for my highest good and greatest joy.

I love my life just exactly the way it is. I am free to make whatever changes are necessary for my future.

I can risk doing what I feel is right.

I am a life enhancer.

I am creating a healthy foundation on which creativity can flourish.

The Sacral Chakra

Element: Water

Archetype: The Emperor/Empress

Sense: taste

Shape: a pyramid

Sound: "Ba" (to be chanted into the Sacral Chakra)

Soul lesson: peace and wisdom

The Sacral Chakra is located midway between the pubic bone and the navel. It radiates energy to the front and back of the pelvis, and is the deep center, the life-spring of our physical well-being and vitality. It is this chakra which links us to creativity, well-being, abundance, and pleasure. According to the degree of openness or suppression we have about ourselves as physical, sexual beings, the flow of energy from the center will vary accordingly and will also be reflected in the state of our health and our level of vitality.

The Sacral Chakra is ruled by water; it is a depository of emotional energy and its archetypical quality is power, represented by the archetype of the Emperor/Empress. This is the energy of abundance and mastery of the material plane. When we focus energy into this chakra through exercise, meditation, or massage, it will enliven and vitalize us, enabling us to experience the warmth and pleasure of physical sensations.

In Sanskrit the Sacral Chakra is called Swadisthana, which translates as "sweetness" or "one's own abode." It is our energetic home, our center. The Chinese call it the Den Tien and in Japanese culture it is called the Hara. This center controls our physical movements and vitality level as well as our emotional states. That is why emotions are so directly linked with our sense of well-being. This center is also responsible for pleasure and money (i.e., prosperity or the lack of it). We will look at these in turn.

Well-Being

This is a state of feeling good about ourselves. This is when harmony resonates between stabilized emotions, a peaceful spirit, clear thinking, and abundant vitality. This sense of harmony gives the experience of happiness and peace.

Well-being arises when we are in tune with ourselves, our environment, and the universe, and it can have a very strong physical manifestation. There is also a state of mind identified with it. All our blocks to feeling good about ourselves become reflected in this chakra.

One of the main dysfunctions of this chakra is greed. At an emotional level this is the awareness that who you are and what you have is insufficient. As a consequence you will want to be or have more in order to compensate for this sense of emptiness. Well-being can also generate precisely the opposite experience. It is the feeling that who you are and what you have or do is enough. There is a deep sense of acceptance involved with this state. When we allow this awareness to permeate our consciousness we become balanced. Our consciousness then pivots on this still point. It is the focal point for action, movement, and expansion, the place from which to move. When we move out towards others or towards action because we feel that we are not enough in ourselves then we can over-extend our energies and deplete our strength. I often see patients with ME[1] struggle with issues around balancing and maintaining energy levels and they often over-stretch themselves. Sometimes they have a need to prove to themselves that they are good enough because they harbor deep-seated feelings of inadequacy. This in itself is exhausting and takes a great deal of energy which could far better be used in the healing process and for creativity.

James is a case in point of a young man who suffered from ME. He had had this disability for five years and had been in and out of work, as well as having suffered disappointment in a long-standing relationship. He developed strong food allergies and cravings for alcohol and dope, both of which weakened him even more.

He was treated over a long period of time with homeopathic remedies and came to see me to work through his underlying sense of failure at not being able to do things which he wanted to do. As we worked to revitalize his Sacral Chakra, it became evident how he would exhaust himself attempting to prove his worth. There was deep, underlying guilt about his sexuality and when he started to address these issues and deal with his angry feelings about being robbed of his sexuality he started to heal very quickly. His whole appearance began to change. He slimmed down, started getting more exercise without punishing himself with tasks which were too tiring. He changed his diet to more wholesome and nutritious food. He took up meditation on a regular basis and was able to empower himself in his work so that he earned more money. His self-worth and self-respect rocketed and he is more soundly anchored in a way of life which gives him both pleasure and purpose.

Both rest and relaxation are essential requirements for personal growth. Without the ability to embrace pleasure in our lives we shrivel, become brittle and dry mentally, emotionally, and physically. Learning to honor our physical form is a function of the Sacral chakra. Making sure that you have enough rest, balanced nutrition, clean air and water, and that your body is cared for with enough exercise, and conscious,

---

[1] Myalgic encephalitis, sometimes known as post-viral fatigue syndrome, or, more commonly, "yuppie flu."

loving touch is essential for your well-being. The positive aspects of this center are that you are well-fed, clean, freshly clothed, and living in conditions which reflect the best of yourself.

Feeling good and looking after yourself can in themselves give great pleasure. People who are wounded emotionally and who then "let themselves go" are disconnecting from their vital source. Depression is literally a closing down of this chakra's energy. How well you look after yourself and manage to get the proper balance of rest, stimulation, exercise, and emotional gratification reflects your degree of essential well-being.

Anything which blocks an adult from maintaining a degree of well-being is usually an issue relating to parenting, or abuse at some early stage of development. If we block off the flow of love and pleasure in our lives then we will continue that self-abusive pattern into relationships, work situations, and our lives in general. This pattern will become part of how we see ourselves.

Pleasure is at the very core of our physical existence. How much pleasure we allow ourselves is an indication of how we value ourselves and how connected we are to our core. Pleasure is what we are at the most fundamental level. When we allow pleasure into our lives it helps us feel good about ourselves. It is a reward for our being. A lack of pleasure is a way in which we punish ourselves.

Many people have the attitude in spiritual work that the body is merely a servant of the mind. They often feel that the body's needs can be neglected and are hostile towards the idea of physical gratification. People who deny the body are often strict on themselves and often have many rules about how life should be. It is unconscious expectations about how life should be that limit our satisfaction and happiness. Life itself is pleasure before it is anything else and to cut ourselves off from the life-force is to deprive ourselves of vitality and energy. Pleasuring is something which needs to be learned in our culture. We honor the mind about all else and give little space for simple pleasures. It is often people from primitive cultures who remind us of life's simple joys and pleasures. Take, for instance, the tradition among Indian mothers who massage their babies for forty days after birth. The child is welcomed through touch and from the beginning is helped to experience himself through his body. He carries an innate sense of belonging and being welcome throughout his life.

In the West we have grouped sexuality and sensuality together. We need to separate these two functions so that we don't violate our precious gift of sexuality in pursuit of strokes and touching which we all need in order to experience happiness and pleasure.

The Sacral Chakra governs both physical vitality and the flow of emotional energy. Well-being is a consequence of expressing our feelings and releasing our emotional energy. Physical well-being is closely linked with our feelings. The desire for pleasure puts us in touch with our fundamental longing for love. Looking after our own needs means knowing what is best for us and expressing how we feel. We need to seek pleasure in order to feel good about ourselves.

Massage reawakens the vital energy of the body. It works at many levels to revitalize us. The Alexander Technique and Cranial Sacral therapy are two techniques which also help achieve a stage of well-being. Meditation and Yoga are practices which can help bring you back to the still point within yourself. Any or all of these help in releasing blocked-up tension.

It is directly through the body that we come to experience pleasure, and through pleasure we get a deeper connection with our true nature. Connecting with pleasure is to get in touch with something fundamental about life. It helps us take stock of our basic beliefs about life. Is it then something we must control or manipulate, or is it something we may readily submit to? Our attitudes surrounding these questions are directly focused in the Sacral Chakra.

This center also incorporates issues of power. Some of the fears and anxieties relating to this chakra also have to do with manipulation. People who are imbalanced in this chakra often have distinctive body structures. They are prone to large, swollen bellies. They are disconnected from their core and often, out of fear, choose manipulation as a form of getting what they want. They don't trust the implicit sweetness of life to give them what they need.

Well-being is reflected in the way you address yourself to the physical world and how well you can look after your physical and emotional needs. Ultimately, well-being is about how you respond to your own impulses and listen to yourself.

Sexuality

In this age of widespread and virulent transmittable sexual diseases we need to look at our integrity in relation to our bodies and our physical and emotional needs. The body is mechanical in that it has repetitive functions. These functions are controlled ultimately, however, by the free flow of energy through the chakras. This energy in turn is controlled by our attitudes. Our vital energy always follows the thoughts we think.

This process is distinctly reflected in the structure of the body with its "language" of unexpressed emotions. If we are rigid about how we allow ourselves pleasure then we will eventually crack open so as to experience our deep need for love and affection. To deny the body's longing for touch and warmth is to increase further those neurotic tendencies of denial. This feeds our negative patterns of unworthiness and anchors us in feelings of being unlovable and unworthy. Denying our need for touch is a way we have of punishing ourselves.

The Sacral Chakra controls sexuality and our reproductive systems. It feeds energy into the pelvic girdle and stimulates hormonal secretions. When there is sexual dysfunction this chakra is impaired. The quality of release and freedom which one can experience sexually is dependent on attitudes about sexuality and how one's need for pleasure is perceived. Attitudes about sexuality are imprinted on to our consciousness by our families, and particularly our opposite-sex parent. Deeply suppressed incestuous longings result in adults acting out their unconscious desires, looking for the perfect version of their parent.

There are few people who allow themselves to look at their sexual projections on to the opposite sex. These projections begin to run our lives when we don't bring them to consciousness. So much of the energy locked into the pelvic region in the area of the Sacral Chakra is tension resulting from locked-up feelings and desires. It often takes therapy or energetic healing to begin to unblock this energy. If not released, it accumulates and creates physical and psychological disturbances.

Our culture has imposed many negative ideas and views about pleasure. The life of the body and its need for pleasure has been undermined by an over-emphasis on sex. The gravity of this imprint translates itself into misunderstanding and misuse of sexual energy. Many people use their sexuality as a means of expressing their need for affection, control, power, love of security and money. It is too seldom an expression of our deep, spiritual nature, a sharing of the essence of our sweetness, loveliness, and gentleness.

Men have long used their sexuality to anchor their personal identities into a macho myth. Part of that myth says a man must be strong, unfeeling, resolute and emotionally impenetrable. When men are open to incorporating the feminine side of their nature into their personality they are likely to generate deep and rich feelings as well as a great deal of pleasure for themselves. Women, on the other hand, have used sex in our culture to gain security; the quintessential notion that women are helpless is still a pervasive myth.

By taking responsibility for their deeply knowing natures women can begin to draw real power to themselves. Their sexuality then becomes a function of their spirituality. AIDS and the threat of other sexually transmitted diseases have dampened the overt sexual freedom which grew up in the 1960s and '70s. It has made people rethink what to do about their sexuality. We are all learning to discriminate between what feels good and what is actually good for us.

Sexuality has the power to put us in touch with the sublime or it can make us feel as though we are no more than objects for others' pleasure. Discrimination means that we learn to vet who we allow into our lives and with whom we share our deepest and most intimate self.

Our sexuality is our own treasure from the Source. Understanding the power of it empowers us and offers us the opportunity to be truly responsible for ourselves. So much confusion, doubt, and dysfunction surround this focal point of our identity. We are sexual beings. When we give away our precious gift of sexuality out of fear of rejection or loneliness, we lose something of our self-esteem. We use sex to get something it was not designed to give us. To learn to express ourselves without having to give ourselves away is an integral part of maturity. It also preserves and protects our energy. The Sacral Chakra becomes congested and blocked when we fail to honor our sensitivity and deeply feeling natures.

Sex is the ultimate pleasurable experience. It is not a means of proving our worth or enhancing our self-esteem. At its highest level it is a reflection of both these qualities. When we let others define us and give us worth we create dependency. Being in charge of your sexuality is also being in charge of where you place your energy. Ultimately it can lead to a greater sense of responsibility for self and a true sense that there is choice involved in letting people into your life. It also means we can choose to let down the barriers to allowing pleasure into our lives. The joy of incarnation or embodiment is to be able to feel, both physically and emotionally. Both are inextricably linked with the Sacral Chakra. If society cannot "make the body right," then it is something we need to do for ourselves. It is a part of our growth, self-acceptance, and individuation. I feel this requires a slowness, gentleness, and tenderness which comes from understanding ourselves and responsibly communicating our needs. These needs are for pleasure, be it good food, exercise, touch, friendship, or the most intimate sexual contact between people. When we give ourselves pleasure we are freely loving ourselves.

Money

Owning our power and taking responsibility for ourselves unavoidably involves issues of prosperity and abundance. The Sacral Chakra is where the energetic manifestation of this consciousness is formed. In life we need love and money to survive. Many people have the attitude that prosperity is not something they can come to terms with. They see money as something bad or negative or as something beyond their grasp. The basic fear is that there will never be enough. This belief in scarcity limits the flow of energy and locks people into a reality which is based on the false and unreal premise that there just isn't enough for them.

As with our attitudes to sex, our negative feelings about money stand between us and the experience of enjoying prosperity. When our attitudes become fixed, rigid, and disempowering they don't serve our highest good and greatest joy.

Part of our growth and development is taking responsibility for money. Do we do what we enjoy as a form of work? Are we in jobs where we are not experiencing satisfaction because of fears about not having enough? Do we let money determine our dreams and ambitions? How well do we handle money? Do we hold on to it too tightly or do we squander it? Do we use it to buy love and approval? Can we be generous to ourselves and those we love? Can we trust that there will always be enough?

There are so many attitudes which get clogged and congested in our energetic system because we don't look to see what limitations we have imposed on our thinking. Often what stands between us and wealth is our view of how much we do or don't deserve. People's fascination with the superficial is a world problem. So many people identify who they are by what they have or haven't got.

"There are no pockets in a shroud," as a friend once pointed out. What endues are acts of love, kindness, and graciousness which reflect a noble spirit. How deeply our discernment runs in this area determines the energetic state of our bodies.

Movements for the Sacral Chakra

The best exercises for opening and balancing the Sacral Chakra are those which free the hips, knees, and ankle joints. The music you use should be rhythmical and sensual. Lambada music from Brazil or Latin American music in general is excellent. It gives the sensual quality of swaying hips and gentle lilting movements. It is also great fun and very pleasurable. The exercises are as follows:

1 Stand with your feet together and knees slightly bent. Begin to rotate the ankles by moving your knees in circles. This will begin to free the ankles. Continue this movement. Bring your hands onto your knees and rotate them in small circles. First move in one direction and then the other.

2 Stand with your feet about shoulder-width apart and your hands on your hips. Gently rotate your hips in circles, first in one direction and then in the other. Move slowly and rhythmically, feeling your hips and legs. Try to stay connected to your breathing as you do this movement.

3 With your hands on your hips and your knees slightly bent, thrust your pelvis forward and backwards. Use your breath to guide you so that you stay connected as your body moves. On the exhale move the pelvis forward and on the inhale swing your pelvis backward.

These exercises will help to increase your sensitivity and strength coordination.

After doing the warming-up exercises allow yourself to move freely to the music. Gently move your pelvis, swaying and rocking freely as you move. You may want to try dancing in front of a mirror where you can see yourself. What are your feelings as you watch yourself move? Do you find this pleasurable or are you self-conscious? Are you critical of yourself? Is your pleasure decreased by your self-criticism? Do you feel that you are not good enough in some way?

Are you willing to find pleasure in watching yourself have fun? When you find yourself diminishing yourself and cutting off the flow of pleasure can you stop and acknowledge what you are doing? Can you release this negative attitude and affirm yourself?

Massage for the Sacral Chakra
As with all the chakra massages, find a warm and comfortable space in which to work. You may wish to have soft music, incense, and a candle burning.

1 Begin the first part of this massage on the front of the body. To locate the Sacral Chakra imagine a point 2 inches below the navel and 2 inches into your pelvis.

2 Now with your right hand begin to spiral energy out of the chakra, moving in a clockwise direction.

3 As the energy feels freer, less tight and tense (after approximately 5 minutes), turn your partner over so they are face down on their stomach.

4 Place your right hand over the Sacral Chakra, palm down, and anchor your left hand somewhere on your partner's back. This keeps the energetic polarity properly balanced.

5 Begin to rub across the chakra, going from hip bone to hip bone right over the sacrum. You can make large circles (moving clockwise), figures of eight, or simply rub back and forth.

6 Ask your partner if the pressure and tempo is alright. It is particularly important in this center, which contains our sense of pleasure, to take responsibility for expressing our likes and dislikes about what feels good to us.

Color of the Sacral Chakra

The Sacral Chakra can be visualized as orange, the color of physical vitality and life energy. People who live out of this center are often very strong physically. They have high levels of energy and seem to be able to sustain robust levels of activity. They seem to rest only when they exhaust themselves. Because these people are so focused on the physical dimensions they often have trouble raising their spirit to higher levels of vibration. They require turquoise or blue as an antidote to this block on the physical plane.

People who live predominantly in this orange energy can be manipulative and cunning. They need to learn to trust the spiritual part of life to sustain them rather than just their own physical energy.

This center controls the free flow of emotions. When Sacral energy moves freely we are open to experiencing ourselves and expressing our feelings. When we dam up the flow of emotional energy this center becomes clogged and congested. People who have experienced abuse or illness often have problems centering within themselves. This is usually a sign of distress and dysfunction in this center.

Physical movement, meditation, and doing those things in life you enjoy will repair a lot of the damage that may have been done to this chakra. It has been demonstrated that when we do things we enjoy our bodies actually register a higher level of hormonal output. When we are happy doing what we enjoy everything about us starts to flow in a more healthy way. Only we can say what gives us joy and allow ourselves to do good things for ourselves.

Healing Uses for the Color Orange

It is good for:
Exhaustion
Intense emotions
Menstrual cramps
Infertility
Arthritis
Mood shifts
Kidney dysfunctions
Revitalization
Depression
Light-deprived states during winter
Respiratory stimulant
Para-thyroid depressant
Thyroid energization
Anti-spasmodic
Carminative
Lungs

Attributes of the Sacral Chakra

Positive	*Negative*
Taste	Greed
Appetite	Manipulation
Desire	Sentimentality
Pleasure	Exhaustion
Pride	Indiscriminate sexuality
Emotion	Guilt
Vitality	
Sexual satisfaction	
Power	
Prosperity	
Discrimination	

Gemstones
Carnelian
Coral
Jasper
Agate
Bloodstone
Hematite
Dolomite

Aromas
Geranium
Sandalwood
Jasmine
Patchouli
Oak Moss Resin
Pine

Questionnaire for the Sacral Chakra

1 What things in life do you feel that you deserve for yourself?

2 Do you feel you are entitled to pleasure and happiness?

3 Do you feel that abundance and prosperity are within the realms of possibility for you?

4 Do you feel that you must always struggle and sacrifice for the things you want?

5 How well do you look after your physical needs?

6 How much permission do you give yourself to feel your feelings?

7 Do you give yourself the rest and relaxation you need?

8 Do you keep yourself clean and attractive?

9 Do you live in an environment which is supportive to your peace and happiness?

10 Do you give yourself time to listen to your needs for peace, harmony, rest and relaxation?

11 How do you honor your sexuality?

12 Do you acknowledge your need for touch and affection?

13 Are you willing to take time for yourself to do what gives you pleasure?

14 Do you do the things which you enjoy?

Affirmations for the Sacral Chakra

I unconditionally love and approve of myself at all times.

I trust in my own perfection.

I am good enough to have what I want.

I release my negative attitudes which block my experience of pleasure.

It is safe to have life easy and pleasurable.

I allow pleasure, sweetness, and sensuality into my life.

I allow abundance and prosperity into my life.

I am in control of my own sexuality.

I give myself permission to enjoy my sexuality fully.

I trust the Infinite Intelligence to give me everything I need for my growth and development.

I am enough. What I do is enough. What I have is enough. Who I am and what I do is enough.

I open myself to the beauty, joy, and harmony of the Universe and I enjoy it.

I trust the process of life.

I love myself exactly as I am right now.

The Solar Plexus Chakra

Element: Fire
Archetype: The Father/The Warrior
Sense: sight
Shape: a sphere
Sound: "Ra" (to be chanted into the Solar Plexus)
Soul lesson: human and divine love

The Solar Plexus Chakra sits underneath the diaphragm, directly below the sternum. It is the center which governs personal power, self-worth, decision-making, and insight. Most people traveling a path towards gathering temporal power have their energy focused here. Nonetheless, everyone on the path to higher consciousness must also come to terms with the issues contained in this chakra.

Self-Worth

The central theme of this center is that of self-worth. Right now on our planet this is a very important issue. Once we are able to balance this center with the experience of our deepest knowing about love, our personal power can be released to help and serve humanity. To be able to transcend the limitations of petty ego puts one in a place of peace, love, and harmony. That place is, of course, the heart.

Given the worldly values held dear by modern-day, civilized cultures, self-worth has come to be linked ever more closely with accumulation of material gain and power. The pressure is always on to possess more things: attain job status, have prestigious experiences, and build ego by way of sexual conquests. Achieving and maintaining a power base to prove one's worth requires a vast amount of energy. The more ruthless the game you need to play out to achieve the illusion of power and control, the more sacrifice of true essence and natural spirit there must be. When we experience that we are whole, complete and perfect just as we are, we are free to stop playing out the games of illusion centered on achievement, acquisition, and separation.

Often personal power issues revolve around inadequacy and a lack of confidence, both limiting to our experience of worth. Many people feel they are not worthy of love, pleasure, joy, happiness, or prosperity. This sense of unworthiness springs from a block to the Solar Plexus Chakra. Many people are in search of a way to latch their identity on to external realities such as possessions. But if we focus our attention on who we truly are, we begin to understand what personal power is really about.

When the energy of the Solar Plexus is balanced, other people cannot make primary decisions about our lives for us. Nor do we lack the self-confidence to take our own lives fully into our own hands. We can break away from ties of dependency to people and situations which undermine our sense of self-worth. Our true worth does not rest on what we have or what we do, or on how others may choose to validate us. It is very difficult to achieve this differentiation in a world like ours powered by money and strong acquisitive urges. To move towards a true state of health comes from love for ourselves.

To acquire an understanding of life's deeper meanings many cultures ritually initiate their young people into the mysteries and magic of life and death. Our sense of self-worth is intact when we know the value of who we are, regardless of how others may see or experience us. This inner knowing, as I have said, can come from various forms of initiation into adulthood and the recognition of responsibilities which go hand in hand with these levels of maturity.

Our culture may not have any formalized initiations; however, the rites of passage from childhood through adolescence into adulthood are inescapably part and parcel of growing up. They are our way of gaining autonomy and greater responsibility. Each stage of life gives us an opportunity to overcome new fears and, by doing so, to contact our inner strengths.

I feel that we subconsciously seek out people and experiences which will help us develop our own inner worth. Such opportunities may sometimes appear in the guise of loss, and our sense of self-worth may develop at the expense of deep personal pain. We may, for example, have to go through losing jobs, breaking up relationships, or going bankrupt to find out that, in essence, we are not those things with which we have hitherto identified. Rather, we are individuals each with unique value of our own. Through these harsh experiences we are able to realize that we amount to much more than any purely material reckoning we may have made.

Sai Baba, the Indian guru, says that when you lose your money and your friends, then you find God, and that is finding yourself. At present on this planet more and more people are having to move out of the comfort zone they have constructed around their material lives because of recession and consequent unemployment. Marriages and relationships previously based on power and abuse are being looked at afresh with an eye to equality and mutual empowerment. The whole fabric of our power-based reality is starting to crumble as more and more energy is channeled to spiritual ends across the planet. People are shifting from an outer-based awareness and moving towards a deep sense of inner knowing.

The energy of this planet and of each individual will shift to a higher octave of consciousness as spirituality embraces ever more people. Many people who were previously too sensitive and unable to cope with third chakra power energy are emerging as healers to help transmute this destructive breakdown of our society into a new form of awareness. In doing this they are finding an entirely fresh sense of self-worth and a deep respect for spiritual essence through being open, sensitive, and vulnerable. They are choosing relationships and careers with an awareness that they themselves are valuable and can make a difference to other. From this innate sense of their self-worth they are beginning to make significant contributions to our society.

Power

Awareness of one's worth quite literally imbues individuals with power: the kind of power which Christ spoke of when he threw the moneylenders out of the temple. it is the personal power of a Martin Luther King, Mother Teresa, and others who, with nothing and because of their willingness to be "nothing," have manifested great change on this planet. Their examples of courage and dignity have taught us all.

What often gets congested in the Solar Plexus Chakra is fear or cowardice. A major part of personal growth and maturity is the initiation into freedom. When we leave behind parental, familiar, or tribal support to seek our own individuation, fear is so often our biggest obstacle. This fear has its roots in early childhood rearing. Very few people are encouraged to become the best they can be, and it is the major challenge of our time, to maximize our God-given talents so desperately needed now by all of us on this planet. This move towards individuation is in fact the crucial spiritual journey for us to make. We have sought love and approval from our families and cultures and in doing so unconsciously we have bought into all their fears and restrictions about how life must be.

Power is the ability to move something or someone. We all need to have the experience of our own power at some point in our development. This awareness gives us the strength to move forward in our own lives. Where so many of us get stuck is in seeking the validation of our being, or our power, from others. Until we can feel and be with our own selves and know our own worth we will constantly be giving over our power to others to validate us or heal us.

Where many people get arrested in their development is in hanging on to people or situations which never give them acknowledgment of their value. This is always disempowering. True acknowledgment is the vehicle we need to urge us forward. And so at certain points in life we need to learn to give it to ourselves and not seek it from external sources. This is where the energy of the Solar Plexus becomes engaged.

The power to create illness and distress is only an inversion of our power to create all the goodness we wish to have in our lives. An awareness of this power comes when we tap into the depths of our own aliveness and begin to understand the nature and purpose of our being.

The books of Carlos Castañeda speak of an old Yaqui Indian sorcerer named Don Juan, who taught Castañeda to understand and respect the nature of power in all living things, both visible and invisible. The acknowledgment of this power, which some call God or Infinite Intelligence, is in itself transforming. It releases us from the sense of victimhood which can spring from circumstances and rockets us up through the archetypes to higher and higher levels of healing and being. Often what blocks this awareness of self is our fear of failure. We often set an invisible standard for measuring our success or failure in life. These judgments of what constitutes failure are often left over from our parents' unfulfilled expectations of life. We take these standards upon ourselves out of love or obligation. Again, these attitudes will enhance or diminish the flow of energy through the Solar Plexus Chakra.

Parents often fail to see the unique expression of individuality within their children. They might neglect this spark of life for conformity's sake, preferring to find acceptance in the eyes of their social group rather than nourish budding, and perhaps eccentric, creativity. This creates a weak Solar Plexus.

When natural gifts and talents become subverted into socially acceptable behavior energy gets locked away and may find instead a very unacceptable channel of expression when the child demands to be seen and heard. We need natural spontaneity, creativity, and power of self-expression to be readily acknowledged for the healthy development of our self-worth. Our greatest gift is to learn to recognize our own worth. When the fear of failure becomes focused in the Solar Plexus this deep negativity may manifest as ulcers, liver or gallbladder trouble, diabetes, or chronic constipation. These can all be the result of deeply suppressed emotions. The organs of digestion and assimilation become affected because, on the psychic plane, fear is blocking the flow of life energy.

The ways in which we experience love and power are clear reflections of how we feel about ourselves. Most people bond together out of fear. They are afraid to be alone or step out into the arena of life to develop and express the full potential of who they are on their own. They fear rejection or humiliation, and attach themselves to the negative because deep down they fear what pleasure, success, and joy may mean. Ultimately it is those positive aspects of life which create freedom and release. Negative attitudes enslave people and prevent them from looking beyond their own self-imposed limitations. So much health and creative energy can become totally dissipated when Solar Plexus energy is dysfunctional.

If we have been made to feel judged as not good enough by our families, churches, or schools, we need to reclaim the value of our own worthiness. Our work lies in the direction of developing love and understanding of ourselves as worthy human beings. This sense of worth needs to be totally independent of what we do or have, our race, religion, size, shape, age, or social position. We are worthy simply because we exist.

Discrimination

One of the essential qualities of the Solar Plexus is its ability to discriminate. At the physical level this is a function of the digestive system and in particular the primary function of the small intestine. This is where food gets taken into the body and assimilated or rejected and passed on as waste to be evacuated. At an emotional level this function is about what and who we choose to make part of ourselves. Just as the small intestine chooses what nutrients the body needs to keep for growth and development so emotionally we choose which experiences to assimilate and which to pass on.

If our attitude towards ourselves is loving and accepting then only experiences which enhance our well-being get taken in, assimilated, and made part of our depository of self-esteem. If, on the other hand, our attitudes about who we are are dependent on external factors, such as what others think of us, or how much money we have, or what size and shape we are, then we will starve ourselves of positive experiences, waiting vainly for someone to validate who we are.

The Solar Plexus relates specifically to inner-knowing. The physical sense which it governs is sight. On a spiritual level it means that we open ourselves to an experience and we see what is ultimately good for us. Do we need to open more and say "yes"? Or do we need to say "No, this is not what I either want or need at this moment in my life"? In so questioning we learn to set the boundaries of our experience. This process is an in-built self-protective mechanism.

It has been said that nothing can hurt you unless you give it the power to do so. The function of discrimination is in part the ability to release people and experiences which diminish your worth. The quintessential point here is to know your worth.

Movement for the Solar Plexus Chakra

Opening the Solar Plexus with movement needs to be very gentle. Start with music which has a flowing sound to it and that you can move to easily and smoothly. It needs to have a melodic quality.

1 Begin the exercises with your feet a foot apart. Take in a deep breath of air and raise your arms out to your sides. Gently start to move them back until they touch behind you. This stretches the diaphragm gently and releases the Solar Plexus. Exhale as you move your arms backwards and expel the stale air from your lungs.

2 The next exercise begins by tucking your hands under your arms and making circles with your elbows. This gently energizes the ribcage and activates the breathing. Blow the air out of your lungs continuously as you do these circles. The lungs fill automatically with air so concentration on exhalation.

3 Standing with the feet turned in, about a food apart, raise your arms gently over your head and tilt your pelvis forwards so that the chest is pushed out. Breathe out through the mouth and keep your head tilted forward. Make sure your gaze is fixed on something in front of you. This begins to energize the body so rapidly that you may begin

to tremble. Keep the eyes straight ahead and open. Breathe out as you do this until you start to feel highly energized. There is no need to hyperventilate. Slow, deep breaths will activate your energy.

Massage for the Solar Plexus Chakra

As always, find a warm, comfortable spot to do your massage. Have a candle, some incense, if you like, and gentle music which will help your partner to relax.

1 Start with your partner lying on their back. Have them take a few deep relaxing breaths to release superficial tension.

2 Begin to draw energy out of the Solar Plexus by making clockwise circles with your right hand. Begin to pull the energy up and out of the plexus. Continue doing this for approximately ten minutes.

3 Turn your partner over so they are lying face down. Locate the plexus point on the spine. It sits directly behind the base of the sternum bone below the ribcage.

4 Begin by rubbing this area gently with your right hand. Make sure the left hand is anchored on the body to ensure the energy is well-polarized.

5 Rub across this area back and forth. You can make figures of eight or circles.

6 Find what level of pressure and tempo is suitable to your partner. Do this massage for approximately twenty minutes.

The Color of the Solar Plexus Chakra

The color of the Solar Plexus is yellow. It is the brightest in the spectrum and the color which contains the most light. The color represents the light of the intellect and wisdom. It is the color of knowing and illumination.

Yellow works on the physical body in the following manner. It loosens, relaxes, and stimulates the eliminative processes. It helps stimulate the brain and aids in clearer and more positive thinking. Yellow works primarily on the digestive functions. It helps loosen congestion in the color for better elimination. It helps eliminate calcium and lime deposits which form around the gallbladder and kidneys. Yellow is also a bone builder. It hardens soft or even broken bones faster and hardens soft bones. It activates the thymus gland for better and more rapid growth in children.

It is also effective in loosening and eliminating the effects of a cold. Yellow and lemon are great enliveners and eliminators. The vibrational frequency of these colors increases the flow of all vital cleansing fluids inducing drainage action throughout the body so that each cell frees up toxins which contribute toward illness. The Solar Plexus radiates energy throughout the body, both physically and psychically. Energy is drawn in through the Solar Plexus and distributed to each chakra. That's why this center is often referred to as the psychic energy pump.

When people live directly from this place of power they will be constantly trying to prove their worth. This means that they will always have to create opposition and inevitably develop a rigid dualistic approach to life. There is me and you, us and them. In order to exercise power the mind needs first to create separation, duality, and opposition. This then translates into attitudes that one is better or worse than someone else. And in this way ideas of self-worth and power become subject to and limited by a perpetual process of comparative judgments.

The fact is that love only has a chance when you know that you are good and worthy simply because you exist, and can desire a real sense of wholeness and completeness, purely from being alive. Human power is limited. As physical creatures we can only achieve limited success. The energy which passes through the Solar Plexus, when it is acting as a divisive filter, will also be diluted when this happens. The energy is first taken in by you and is then projected on to those you see in opposition to yourself so as to maintain your illusion of power.

When we say "own your power" it means take back what is yours rather than projecting your power on to others, such as parents, teachers, authorities, doctors, or therapists. Real power is a consequence of being responsible for yourself, your own actions, and your own emotions.

The Solar Plexus Chakra is also the center for astral projection and is sensitive to astral influences, as well as being receptive to spirit guides and being a spur to psychic development. Where there is too much yellow around or the Solar Plexus is opened too wide, there can be disharmony, nervousness, digestive disruption, and eating disorders. There will also be psychic and mental disorder. With too little yellow, or the chakra dysfunctional you get apathy, tiredness, mental stagnation, obesity, and lack of psychic balance. Balance in this center creates self-confidence, emotional stability, inner peace, and efficient use of nourishment and energy. The Solar Plexus is in a very strong sense our bridge to other people.

We are connected to people we both love and hate through the energy of the Solar Plexus. We are vulnerable to people because we are open in our energetic field. Learning to balance our inner and outer knowledge is part of balancing the Solar Plexus.

Healing Uses for the Color Yellow
It is good for:
Vitalization
Mood elevating
Dispelling fears
Helping exhaustion
Digestion
Constipation
Psychic development
Motor stimulation
Lymphatic activation
Catharsis
Building up nerves

Lemon (a component color) acts in the following ways:
Cerebral stimulant
Antacid
Laxative
Expectorant
Bone-building

Attributes of the Solar Plexus Chakra

Positive
Intelligence
Balance
Nourishment
Strong nerves
Personal power
Self-confidence
Self-respect
Assimilation on physical

Flexibility
Decisiveness

Negative
Fear of failure
Inability to make decisions
Poor judgment
Lack of confidence
Low self-respect
Apathy
Rigidity
Poor assimilation
and psychic levels

Gemstones
Topaz
Citrine
Amber
Peridot
Tiger's Eye
Yellow Fluoride

Aromas
Rose oil
Lemongrass
Lemonbalm
Amber
Aloes
Juniper

Questionnaire for the Solar Plexus

1 How well-developed do you feel your confidence in yourself is?

2 How well-developed do you feel your sense of self-worth is?

3 Do you respect yourself at all times? Where does your sense of self-respect need developing?

4 Are you able to discriminate between what feels good and what is actually good for you?

5 Do you express your anger and other strong emotions?

6 Do you listen to your deepest insights about people and situations?

7 Do you trust what you feel to be right?

8 Are you easily influenced by others?

9 How developed is your sense of self-love?

10 Do you value your abilities? Your talents and personal gifts?

11 Are you threatened by a sense of failure?

12 In what areas does your confidence need boosting?

13 Are you willing to release negative attitudes about yourself?

Affirmations for the Solar Plexus

I deeply love and approve of who I am.

I am worthy of my own-self-love.

I love and respect myself at all times.

I trust in love.

I trust my worthiness.

I am worth my weight in gold.

There are no failures. I learn from everything I do.

I believe that everything is for my highest good and greatest joy.

I love life.

I listen to and trust my deepest insights.

I am worthy of the very best in life.

I release judgment and let my life flow.

The Heart Chakra

Element: Air

Archetype: The Fool

Sense: feeling and touch

Shape: heart inside crescent moon

Sound: "Ha" (to be chanted into the Heart Chakra)

Soul lesson: brotherhood and love

The Heart Chakra is the beginning of the path to higher consciousness and light. It relates to the soul lesson of brotherhood. It also stimulates the sense of touch and feeling. The emotional issues which revolve around it are called transpersonal, as they relate to the aspect of the Self which goes beyond the limitations of the ego to higher issues of love and unity. Transpersonal issues relate to our experience of communion with another. The first three chakras we explored are concerned with tribal, family, and personal issues of survival. These center on ground-edness in the material world and the power we harness to live in and interact with the world of matter. Once we move to the Heart Chakra we se out on the path of the spirit.

Unconditional Love

This chakra is located to the right of the physical heart. It balances the physical heart's energy. Within its energy are held joy, bliss, brotherly love, and compassion. There is also the capacity for serenity, peace, and a deep longing for connection. This energy is not about sexuality, exploitation, or dependency. It revolves around our capacity to give and receive love purely and unconditionally.

Within the realm of the Heart Chakra is the understanding and experience of our innate worth. We are born innocent, good, and pure. Whatever the reasons which have led us to close our hearts it is essential that we now reawaken to our need for love. If there was only love in our lives we would never develop, mature, or evolve. Our spirituality would lack the dimension of free choice to connect with our deep inner knowing. Love has a chance when we choose to transcend our small-minded judgments and criticism. Otherwise, we would never be conscious of the healing which comes with true forgiveness.

The Heart Chakra is the pathway to the realm of spirit in which all God's creatures are one and where love is eternal and unconditional. Our life experiences are meant to teach us the reason and purpose for our being: I believe it is to learn about love.

Many people feel they have not had enough love in their lives. Material pressures, narcissistic vanity, or strong ego ambitions have robbed many people of the desire for love. We have replaced our basic spiritual understanding of unconditional love with ideas that if we had more, looked better, were younger, or were more highly paid then we would get the love we wanted. It is a perverse circle which ultimately takes us back to looking into ourselves.

Within our own hearts we are able to find and nurture our spirit. More and more people today seem to understand the need for unconditional love. Many people have been raised in families where attainment was a prerequisite for getting any affection or kindness. We are often uncomfortable with this idea and the responsibility it implies. If, however, we were to feel that we were loved unconditionally then we would have to drop our petty acts of vengeance or self-sabotage, our nastiness, and our grievances. We would then o pen ourselves to love. We would also have to give up our lust for power and deal with our greed. This is what it means to surrender to the healing power of love.

Often enough we buy into other people's negative ideas about how we should be. We may feel we do not deserve love or that God has forsaken us because, in some way, we haven't "measured up." Some people may have struggled in very insecure homes where love was only available on very conditional terms. The lack of genuine love in our lives makes us neurotic and suspicious of the real thing when we are faced with it. Very few people today would have the capacity to recognize the unconditional love Christ offered, for instance. And yet, ironically, this unconditional love is what we seek and long for in our hearts.

When we are around people with open Heart chakras there is such a strong feeling of acceptance and lightness. The need to perform, be something or someone other than what we truly are, simply evaporates. In its place comes joy, pleasure in the moment, and a sanctity of spirit which uplifts and releases all negativity. People with open Heart Chakras show us the path to forgiveness. They ease our burdens and help us feel truly worthy of love and affection. We don't feel the need to work hard to prove our worth. Instead we experience that we are lovable and worthy. This is the energy in which we blossom and our true gifts begin to emerge. Without the quality of this energy in our lives at some time our spirits shrink and we never make our precious God-given gifts and talents truly available to the world.

This quality of unconditional love does not have to come from family. Indeed, it may come in the least suspected way. Perhaps it comes from a friend, therapist, guru or teacher, or even from someone we barely know. What is important is that at some time we are given the opportunity to know that we are lovable. From that moment the impediments to experiencing our true selves begin to drop away.

Opening the Heart

There are times, through bearing witness to great misery or human suffering, that we have the opportunity to know the goodness of the human heart. Witnessing brotherly love opens our eyes and our hearts to the graciousness the human spirit is capable of attaining. The Heart Chakra signifies the point in human evolutionary development where a person may choose to go within himself and open his heart to love. There may be specific circumstances which propel a person to this level of consciousness. Falling in love, great loss or emotional pain involving a loved one, seeing the birth of a child, even a simple or gracious gesture can stimulate the heart to open in wonderment and joy. It may be a very spontaneous experience, such as when someone reaches out to us in our suffering, which helps us to open our hearts. One thing is sure: at some point before we die we will all engage our hearts in an act of love.

We may need to ask for forgiveness for the hurt we have caused ourselves and others before our hearts can open fully. The more we desire to live in the light of love the more we will be given the opportunity to do so. Releasing the blocked pain that comes from not having had enough love in our lives is essential in order to let the heart open fully and expand our capacity to love now. Only with love is there likely to be healing. Without love we wither.

We each have our unique lessons to learn about love. The forms which this opening of the heart takes are as varied as each individual. What is experienced, however, is the knowledge that we are one with all people in our need for love. This deep sense of brotherhood is what unites us, gives us strength and, ultimately, healing.

The awareness that love is within us is beautifully illustrated by a story that my teacher and master, H. W. L. Poonja, tells. Poonja is now in his eighties. He is a physically vigorous and intellectually astute person. He is an ardent disciple of Sri Ramana Maharshi, the acclaimed Indian saint and spiritually enlightened teacher who died in the late 1940s. Poonja spent many years traveling and teaching about the Source within each of us.

He tells a wonderful story about how he was once visiting a holy man who lived in a cave in southern India. This man told Poonja that his cave gave him pure joy, contentment, and peace. He felt that he would never be able to live anywhere else because the cave was the source of his happiness. Poonja told me how he laughed at this story. He told the man that the cave was very simply rock and dirt. The qualities he had projected into the stone were inside him and that he could carry these qualities anywhere he went in life. His external reality was only a reflection of his inner state of being.

Relationships, possessions, and work start to take on a new lightness and perspective when we begin to live from this space of love without ourselves. Everything then becomes a reflection and expression of our deepest knowing about love. We become the source of the love in our lives rather than making outer reality responsible for the love we need.

It is easy to make others wrong and to blame them for not doing things for us in the way we would like. There is no shortage of things to complain about in life. On the other hand we can choose to establish a new order of relating to ourselves, to people around us, to animal life and nature by knowing and acknowledging ourselves as the source of love. All life is formed out of the same consciousness. We open ourselves to the relatedness of all life when we center in our hearts and allow love to flow through us.

Acceptance

The understanding that we are all worthy of love begins with the acceptance of our own love for ourselves. This, in truth, is only a reflection of God's love for us. Acknowledging our vulnerability, innocence, and goodness may be the most difficult and important thing we can do for ourselves. Accepting our weakness gives us strength. Accepting who we are means we accept that we are worthy of our own love. I feel that it is our choice to love. Throughout our lives we may need to renew this choice for it is very easy to fall into negative patterns which stimulate or create resentment, hatred, guilt, and fear. There can always be a reason not to love, to stay hard or unforgiving. It has been said that everything is either love or a call for love.

I think that we have to really ask ourselves if it is worth holding on to our negativity? Do we want love in our lives? We choose love when we acknowledge our feelings, when we stay open and communicate, when we release guilt. The point is to move beyond our feelings once they have become conscious. If we are afraid to feel we will be stuck with unexpressed emotions, which only serve to block our capacity to experience love.

Grief is inimical to the human experience. When prolonged and unexpressed it can be damaging to our lives. Western culture allows us little time to properly mourn a loss. How ironic that is at the present time when there is so much for which to mourn and grieve. So many people have been injured in wars, by drugs, and through debilitating diseases. With the onslaught of these devastating experiences we are being asked to feel the pain, open our hearts, and reach out to give assistance and comfort.

Many people who seemed beyond the pale of society, such as racial minorities, prisoners, HIV and AIDS patients, are demanding to be listened to and loved unconditionally. They are asking us to open our hearts. These bonds help unite humanity. They help us form a brotherhood which is based on respect for differences. Part of this respect carries with it an acceptance of people's pain and grief. This acceptance helps us open our awareness to our hearts.

Traditional Chinese acupuncture speaks about the Heart Protector. This ancient system rightly acknowledges the heart as the most vital functioning organ of the physical body. The emotions associated with the heart are to do with love and they are the most central feelings involved in human life.

The Heart Chakras is highly vulnerable and any abuse to the system with drugs, medicine, or emotional stress will weaken the Heart Chakra and consequently, the heart itself. So it is vital to keep our hearts physically and emotionally pure.

The negative aspects of the Heart Chakra show up as fear of scrutiny, shame, and enmity towards others. This negativity congests the heart's purity and stops the flow of love. People who are blocked around the heart will always be suspicious and critical when love presents itself in their lives. The mind has the facility of turning love away when it presents itself, if we feel we are not deserving. It also has the spiritual capacity to ennoble love and be creative with it. We need love as much as we need food.

It is often the case that open-hearted people have suffered from tragedy, illness, or abuse. They seem to have a deeply felt compassion for others and a true understanding of the nature of suffering. It is important to empower love and to see life's experiences as learning and development for the enrichment of the soul.

There is a saying, "What comes from the heart touches the heart." It is our basic nature to love and it is love which heals all wounds. Love acknowledges the miracle of who we are. The experience of love taps into the true core of life.

The love of God lives within the hearts of each and every one of us. Appeal to the goodness and the light to cleanse our hearts and to purify our spirits so that each of us may fulfill our truest purpose in life.

Movements for the Heart Chakra

The following movements will help you to open the chest and expand the rib cage and lungs. They will help release tension from the heart area. Select music which is peaceful and harmonic.

1 Begin by standing with your feet about a foot apart. Raise your arms above your head, lean back and push your pelvis forward. This will automatically expand your chest. Breathe deeply and release your breath through your mouth, relaxing your jaw and chin. Do this for six inhalations and exhalations. Keep your eyes open and your head forward, otherwise you may get dizzy.

2 Lying on your back on the floor, place your hands under your waist and raise up on to your elbows. Allow your head to fall back between your shoulder blades. As you inhale your chest will expand with air. Breathe in and out six times emphasizing your exhalation through your mouth. Draw the breath in slowly and deeply, release it slowly.

3 Staying in this position, gently ease your head back on to the floor so that your neck is arched and the crown of your

head is touching the floor. Use your elbows to perch your weight on. Take in a breath of air through your nose and emphasize the exhalation through your mouth. Do this for six breaths. Again, do this slowly and consistently.

4 Sitting on your knees with your heels under you, slowly but strongly blow the stale air out of your lungs bending forward as you do so. Keep blowing breaths of air out of the lungs until they feel empty. When your lungs are empty, hold your breath for as long as you can until the lungs start to take in air on their own. Repeat this five more times.

5 Standing with your arms raised to the sides of your body, begin to twist to one side while you force the air out of your lungs. Exhale through the mouth. Twist to the other side and repeat the exercise of emptying the air from your lungs.

Massage for the Heart Chakra

There is a very important point in working on the Heart Chakra. *Never* work directly on the heart. It is too sensitive and responsive to direct touch. In doing this energetic work we shift energy in the following ways.

1 Have your partner lying on their back. Make sure they are warm and comfortable. You may wish to have a candle, incense, and soothing music playing while you do this delicate and sensitive work. Be as gentle and conscious as possible in this most delicate and powerful of centers.

2 Begin by pulling energy from your partner's left shoulder, across the inside of the left breast to their Solar Plexus. This way you are taking energy out of the thoracic cavity and opening the energy out through a stronger channel. Repeat this movement for approximately five minutes.

3 Turn your partner on to their front. There are two places above and below the heart which are used in the Heart Chakra massage.

(a) The first is just above the diaphragm on the back. This is where we give out heart energy. Move your right hand gently across the breadth of the back here repeatedly for ten minutes. You can use back and forth motion, figures of eight, or circles. Be gentle and soft in your touch.

(b) Just below the neck on the upper part of the back is the second place for working on the Heart Chakra. This is where we receive heart energy. Again, with your right hand move back and forth across the tops of the shoulders. You can be very soft and gentle in your touch. Move slowly and feel tension being released here.

The Colors of the Heart Chakra

The colors of the Heart Chakra are pink and green. They relate specifically to the peace and harmony of nature and the joy and gentleness of warm, nurturing love. Together they radiate beauty. Green acts as a purifier and disinfectant in healing. It is the color which symbolically and functionally signifies renewal. Green represents balance in the in-flow and out-flow of energy. Nature loves a lover. She is always willing to be creative and she has chosen green to represent her essence. "Green" people are heart people. They have an affinity for plants and nature. They are generous people with good minds and are sympathetic to others. People come to them with their problems. They enjoy children. They are emotionally balanced, but because they have an open, soft energy they are very prone to hurt. Green is a combination of the wisdom of yellow and the truth of blue.

Green helps people feel better in both spirit and in physical health. It soothes the nerves and gives peace and quiet to the mind, rest and recuperation to the injured body. One can even obtain physical strength from proximity to green. It is a tonic for the spirit.

Pink is the color of love and joy. This is the gentle quality and sweetness of heartfelt love. Pink is warm and reflects the ability to care for oneself and for others. It signifies universal, mother love. And it's interesting that as men begin to open to their feminine nature so pink has become fashionable in men's clothing. It is a color that is fun and lively without being harsh or aggressive.

Healing Uses for the Color Green
It is good for:
Soothing the spirit
Soothing the nerves
Sunburn
Love loss
Loneliness
Harmony and balance
Refreshing
Calming the fear of death
Antiseptic
Emotional stability
Pituitary stimulation
Disinfectant
Germicide
Muscle and tissue building

Attributes of the Heart Chakra

Positive	Negative
Love for self and others	Fear of scrutiny
Empathy	Hatred
Healing	Avarice
Individuality	Selfishness
Brotherhood	Meanness
Unity	Malice
Adaptability	Resentment
Generosity	Callousness
Nobility of Spirit	
Purity	
Gentleness	
Innocence	

Gemstones
Jade
Malachite
Adventurine
Tourmaline
Emerald
Diamond
Green Agate
Peridot

Aromas
Lilac
Violet
Rose
Elemi

Questionnaire for the Heart Chakra

1 Is love at the core of your life?

2 What things about yourself do you love? Do you have a sense of your own loveliness?

3 What things about yourself do you truly enjoy?

4 Who are the people you love and are truly grateful for in your life? What do you love about each of them?

5 Do you remember a time when you felt deeply loved? Do you remember a time you felt deep love for someone?

6 How do you express your love to others?

7 What experiences have helped you to love yourself and others?

8 Have there been people in your life who have helped you to experience love more fully?

9 Who in your life has loved you unconditionally?

10 Who have you loved unconditionally?

11 Are there people you need to forgive in order to open your heart?

12 Are you willing to release anger and resentment so that there is more love available to you?

13 Can you forgive yourself for the times you have not been loving to yourself or to others?

14 Would you like more love in your life? Could you allow it into your experience?

Affirmations for the Heart Chakra

I deeply and truly love and approve of myself.

I am adequate at all times to do that which is required of me.

I love who I am.

I am willing to love everything about myself.

I trust in love.

I open my heart to love.

I forgive myself

I forgive those who need forgiving for not being what I wanted them to be.

I acknowledge my own loveliness.

I am pure, good, and innocent.

Love is the purpose of my life.

Love is everywhere.

I open myself to the healing powers of love.

I follow the path of the heart.

I am confident that the healing power of God's love will heal my mind, heart, and body.

The Throat Chakra

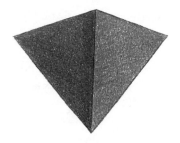

Element: Ether

Archetype: Hermes, the god of communication and messenger between man and the gods

Sense: hearing

Shape: inverted pyramid, directing energy towards the heart

Sound: "Ga" (to be chanted into the Throat Chakra)

Soul lesson: expressing divine will

The Throat Chakra is the center which relates to creative expression and both physical and spiritual will power. It lies in the middle of the throat and feeds energy to the entire neck and jaw area. It energizes the vocal apparatus, the jaw, mouth, teeth, and tongue. It also nourishes the deep brain and brain stem. Tension in the occiput bones at the back of the head often indicates suppressed emotional energy. Suppressed anger, which lodges at the back of the neck and suppressed tears, at the front of the throat, are the primary emotional throat blocks. Either can be indicative of a dysfunctional Throat Chakra.

This center is the most delicate and vulnerable chakra in the human energy system. It is, as a consequence, the center most easily unbalanced by stressful emotional experience or by substance abuse. If the will is not developed to cope with emotional strain and uncertainty the Throat Chakra can easily become congested with emotional energy.

Nearly all addictive habits pass through the Throat Chakra. Smoking, over-eating, alcoholism, and both medical and recreational drugs are ingested through the mouth and throat. These habits not only pollute and diminish our vital energy on the physical level, they corrupt and destroy our creative energy. Negativity in the form of gossip, criticism, cursing, and boasting can all impair the healthy Throat Chakra. The development of will power, when coupled with creative visualization, acts as a thrust to our intentional creative activity and serves to enhance the healthy function of this chakra.

Our ability to visualize what we wish to draw to us, a function of the Brow center, is tempered by our will power. The will acts as a harnessing gear to help us focus our intentionality on what we want to have in our lives. It helps us to channel creative energy into whatever we wish to manifest for ourselves. When we block our emotional expression, either by not saying what we feel or what we want, then we limit our ability to expand into the creative realms of life.

Self-Expression

The Throat Chakra acts as the conduit between the heart and the mind. Through our desire to create and express ourselves, our individuality is strengthened and fortified. Energy which is blocked in the Throat Chakra can be heard in the quality of resonance in the voice itself. The voice can take on the energy of any chakra in its ability to mirror the source of our energy.

When we speak from the Root Chakra the voice can be droning, monotonous, and officious; it will come over as dispassionate and matter of fact, rather like a person expressing a clear fact without any emotional content. When the voice is connected to the Sacral Chakra, it is warm and can have a sexual, seductive quality to it.

When the voice is linked to the Solar Plexus it reflects our personal power. When the voice comes from the heart it carries within it the vibration and essence of love. People who speak from their heart have deep resonating voices that can move us to tears by the quality of their compassion. The voice which is connected to the Brow Chakra may sound dry, cool, and detached. It reflects the sound of detached intellect at work.

The voice is a clear channel of energy which expresses who we are at every level. The voice may sound tight and "held up," which can often be an indication of repressed sexuality. It may have overtones of anger or hatred which tell us to keep our distance from someone. It can sometimes be useful to drift away from your conscious mind to experience the emotional energy someone is imparting rather than the words they are saying.

It is from the Throat Chakra that we express our personal truths. If we swallow our feelings our neck and throat may often show signs of suppressed energy. We may have chronic colds, sore or stiff necks, swollen glands, or repeated loss of voice. Often stiff necks or tight chords or tension down the side of the throat indicate unexpressed anger. Tears can get held in the front of the throat and are all too easily hidden or swallowed.

Often a lump in the throat will be a sign of fear or suppressed hysteria: medically this is termed hysteria globus. People who withhold the truth often develop flabby necks. Inflated or swollen necks tell a story of unexpressed feelings. Good, open communicators have beautiful necks and throats well into advanced years when most people would expect the neck to deteriorate.

Again, energy follows thought and when we express our aliveness and beauty this is physically reflected in the quality of our skin tone, muscle, and vocal resonance. At the moment when emotional energy turns to physical symptoms in the form of pain, inflammation, discharges, or lumps, it is useful to pay attention to the wisdom of the body. This suggests it is the moment to begin expressing suppressed feelings.

Not to express ourselves is to limit our participation and enjoyment of life. Without song, painting, poetry, and dance the finer qualities of our culture would be lost. Through expression of joy and love we find outlets that open the hearts and minds of the people we are around. The throat center is the major chakra for this expression. Feelings which get stuck in the body because they are unexpressed clog up the channels which help us individuate and develop.

The more we allow ourselves a form of personal expression the more we have evidence of who we are and what our purpose is in being here. When we arrive at a level where we accept the validity of our own feelings we also begin the natural process of taking responsibility for our lives. We start to eliminate unnecessary projection of our emotional energy onto other people. We start to express our totality in appropriate ways which reflect back to us greater qualities of energy, higher levels of personal responsibility, and a clear and strong degree of self-empowerment.

How we feel about ourselves can actually be determined by the language we use to express ourselves. There is a large degree of blame and disempowerment in the sentence: "He hurt me." There is more awareness and a sense of insight in the phrase: "It was very hurtful." We always have a choice to empower ourselves and this is clearly reflected in the words we choose.

What language we do choose to express our thoughts and feelings can be replete with unexpressed feelings. Language can either disempower or empower us. What we say directly reflects the degree of responsibility we are willing and able to take for our life experiences. When language demonstrates a high level of awareness and responsibility, it also allows a person to center their own energy within themselves, own and experience their feelings and ultimately to discharge the pent-up emotions this experience has created for them. Once we express this stored-up energy we are then given an opportunity to distill this experience into life-wisdom. This is the function of the Brow Center.

At the ultimate level of responsibility there is true acknowledgment that we create every situation in our lives for our learning, development, and growth. How we experience this learning is expressed in the wisdom of our words. Our integrity is expressed in what Native Americans call "Walk Your Talk." This means to express yourself from your deepest place of truth.

We own our energy and communicate our feelings by coming from a place within us which fully admits responsibility for our experiences. If your experiences have been invalidating and you have let yourself become disempowered it may take time and practice to learn to express how you are feeling from your core. Our emotions come from deep within us. They can express profound beauty and a great sensitivity of spirit. When we honor our feelings we acknowledge our worth and their value.

Creativity

Many people go through life feeling they have nothing worth saying. They may feel that no one cares deeply enough or that it would be inappropriate for them to expose their feelings. In such cases the emotional energy then goes back into the body, and if it stays unexpressed it gathers an additional energetic charge and becomes magnified in intensity. This accumulated energy will eventually seek expression and if not experienced on the emotional level is likely to turn into physical pathology. What then happens is that feelings become far more amplified than they were initially. Unexpressed anger turns to hatred and rage; sadness held in turns to grief. Often this happens when we allow our critical judgment to get in the way of our natural creative expression.

Creativity is a necessary outlet for people who have reservation or difficulty expressing their emotions. Our basic nature is creative and if we cannot manifest this in a natural emotional form then outlets which reflect our feeling state become an important substitute.

Few of us are comfortable showing raw anger or outrage directly. These feelings often need to be channeled into a clear energetic form such as a hobby, sport, or creative project. We may sense there is a great deal of pent-up energy in our blocked emotions and that our friends, families, colleagues, or therapists could not possibly take this overflow. When this happens creativity becomes a lifeline for expressing ourselves and being heard.

The Throat Chakra rules the sense of hearing. This specifically relates to how well we can listen to our own inner voice and hear our own inner rhythms. When the Throat Chakra is open we begin to reach for and touch realms of the spirit. Our true nature wants expression and often this will lead us to a creative endeavor.

The Throat Chakra also relates to the use and development of our will. The use of the will affects the deepest layers of our core. If we have used the will to block our natural impulses to differentiate or distinguish ourselves as individuals we need to temper and soften ourselves with love, gentleness, and understanding. This again relates to the management of our vital energy and is ultimately linked with how we want to live our lives.

There is a direct connection between the suppression of our emotions and what we put into our mouths. The mouth is the opening where we take in the material substance of the world into our bodies. We can choose to put in junk food, dope, alcohol, smoke, or allopathic medicines. All these forms of substance abuse damage our vitality and weigh down the spirit, which might otherwise soar to great and creative heights by way of personal expression.

The Throat Chakra is also the gateway to the center of our sexuality. The energetic link between the pelvis and the throat is strong. Singers are taught to work from the base of their pelvis, anchoring their breath there so as to draw on its immense storehouse of power. Once the throat is open, energy can pass freely into the pelvis; this enlivens sensations and stimulates sexual feelings. It may be that the fear of these feelings is one of the reasons the throat gets shut down in early childhood.

The Throat Chakra acts as the bridge between the spirit of the heart and the conscious mind. It is, in fact, the most immediate channel of expression for our individuality. Through speech we express who we are, reach out for others, express our needs and sentiments and speak up for ourselves in the form of ideas and concepts.

We express ourselves from an early age through acts of defiance and negation. Our ability to say "no" suggests to others that we have distinct feelings, tastes, and ideas. Unfortunately, the Throat Chakra gets shut down at an early age by family, schools, and religious institutions controlling and censoring our creativity and emotional expression. When the Throat Chakra becomes dysfunctional because of limits placed on our personal expression, then disease patterns such as colds, sore throats, chronic tonsillitis, and ear infections follow. Problems with speech and dental problems all reflect limitations of expression. If we think of the teeth alone as an expression of our ability to "take a bite" out of life, then their state of health illustrates how well the language of the body reflects our inner wisdom and existential truths.

Life energy must go somewhere and when there is a block to creative expression it will find an outlet. Musical instruments may become your "voice." Writing stories or plays may help a person display his or her imagination. Paintings and designs can express the part of us which is tied to the wonder and magic of creation itself.

Sports and outdoor pursuits help us to express our inner strengths and vent our pent-up aggression in legitimate and pleasurable ways. Through the narrow passage of the Throat Chakra energy gets focused and honed by the will. Abuse of drugs and alcohol are clear indications of a person's pain and serve only to suppress its expression. In her book, *Witness to the Fire*, Linda Schierse Leonard speaks of the transmutation of pain into a life-enhancing, creative process. Her story is riveting, intense, and challenging. She tells of her battle with alcohol abuse, which reached such staggering levels of deterioration that she nearly died after having lost her family, home, and several jobs. By turning her intense pain into a form of expression through writing she managed to develop enough self-esteem and sense of worth through her creative gifts to become free of her self-destructive tendencies.

I have worked with several creative people who have suffered from blocked Throat Chakras. They desperately need to learn how to manage their energetic output, find good and supportive friends and counselors who they can trust to be there for them and with whom they can honestly express their feelings. At some point in their development it seems there was a deep cutting off of feeling and, most importantly, communication. In some cases parents were too busy or not concerned enough for their development or simply didn't have time to listen. These people as children turned to other forms of expression and are, in some cases, brilliant in their artistic expression. Creativity has become the outlet they needed to live out their unexpressed emotions. This is their source of survival until they can transmute this creativity into a higher spiritual flame. It is through this expression that the world becomes a safe and benign place for them to inhabit.

Movement for the Throat Chakra

Choose gentle, soothing flute or woodwind instrumental music to move to. Gentle Indian ragas are calming and soothing.

1 Begin by standing firmly grounded with feet shoulder-width apart. Drop your chin on to your chest and close your eyes. Free the jaw so that the chin hangs loose on your chest. Breathe in through the nose and let yourself surrender to this restful pose for 30 seconds or more.

2 Now gently roll your head back as far as it will go, resting the back of your head on your shoulders. Drop the jaw again so that the chin is free and take several deep breaths in through the mouth. Close your eyes and rest in this pose for 30 seconds.

3 Now roll your head gently to one side and again free the jaw so that the chin hangs loose and free. Take a breath in through your mouth, close your eyes and rest in this pose for 30 seconds. Repeat, rolling your head to the other shoulder.

4 Gently breathing in, you can start to make head rolls. Expel the breath through your mouth as you slowly roll your head around. As you start to come around, begin to take in air through your nose and release it through your mouth. Repeat this exercise three times. This is best done slowly and easily. Do not force the head around.

5 This next exercise will open your throat and your pelvis. I suggest you try this in a space where you feel comfortable and can make some noise. It is best done where you feel free to express yourself.

(a) Lie on the ground on your back with your knees up and your arms out to your side. Have the palms of your hands facing down. Now take a large inhalation of air. Begin to exhale as you allow your head to fall backwards, your knees to open to the side, and your arms to twist around so that your palms are facing upward.

(b) As you exhale allow a sound to come from the deepest part of your body. At first this may feel awkward. It is, however, deeply releasing and can give you a tremendous sensation of lightness and well-being.

(c) After you have released your breath and you are open, start to close up by bringing your head down, twisting your arms around so the palms are again facing down. Bring your knees together. Repeat this five times and each time you do allow a deeper, richer sound to come from your body. This exercise will soften the throat and allow you to connect your voice to the deepest part of your being.

Massage for the Throat Chakra

Many people are very sensitive to being touched around their throat areas. This part of the body is vulnerable and sensitive. At the same time, there may be a great deal of tension and rigidity which wants to be released.

1 As always, find a warm and comfortable place to do this massage. Light a candle, burn incense, if you wish, and play some gentle, soothing music.

First, using both of your hands, gently massage around the jaw, chin, and cheeks of your partner. Ask your partner to take several deep, releasing breaths. Have them lie back, close their eyes, and begin to settle into a comfortable position. Ask your partner to let their eyes all back into the back of their head and to let their tongue fall back into the back of their throat.

2 Once the face feels relaxed and the jaw is free, begin to draw out congested energy from the front of the Throat Chakra. Use a feather-light touch to make circles; always moving in a clockwise direction and always using your right hand. Pull the energy out and flick it away. A candle and incense will help to purify the energy. Do this for approximately 10–15 minutes.

3 Now turn your partner over. Ask them to rest their fore-head in their hands so that you can gently massage their neck. The back of the neck and occiput is often very congested and blocked in people. Using your right hand on the neck and your left hand gently anchored over the crown area of the head, begin to massage back and forth across the neck and the occiput. If the top of the shoulders are particularly blocked use this same massage technique to rub back and forth across this area to help release tension. Do this for up to 30 minutes.

The Color of the Throat Chakra
The color of the Throat Chakra is turquoise or pale blue. The North American Indian and Tibetan cultures honor and value the stone turquoise above all else. One interpretation for its revered status is that this stone was thought to carry within it the colors of heaven combined with the solidity of earth. It embodied two elements in one, color and substance, air and earth. People whose Throat Chakras are blocked benefit from wearing turquoise, either as the color, such as in a scarf around their neck, or as the stone itself.

When it is coupled with yellow it forms the colors of the rays of low. Together with orange or terracotta it links Sacral Chakra (emotional energy) with the creative expression of the throat. Many sacred paintings and churches are painted these colors, exemplifying the balance of earthly and spiritual energies.

Healing Uses for the Color Turquoise
It is good for:
Soothing painful throats
Strengthening the vocal apparatus
Promoting creativity
Balancing strong earth energies
Cooling burns
Sleep
Headaches
Decreasing swellings and all inflammations
Vitality building

Attributes of the Throat Chakra

Positive	Negative
Communication	Unclear Communication
Articulate speech	Suppressed or "swallowed" feelings
Artistry and craftsmanship	Untruthfulness
Spirituality	Exaggeration
Sincerity	Gossip
Truthfulness	Dependency
Independence	Lack of creative expression

Gemstones
Turquoise
Blue Agate
Blue Topaz
Aquamarine
Crysophase

Aromas
Ylang Ylang
Lavender
Aniseed
Blue Chamomile
Elemi

Questionnaire for the Throat Chakra

1 Do you feel you have a right to express yourself honestly?

2 Do you allow yourself to express your feelings?

3 Are you aware that you suppress your feelings?

4 Do you feel that you have a developed will power?

5 How creative are you?

6 Do you allow yourself to express the creative part of your self? How do you do this?

7 Do you use substance abuse as a way of avoiding your feelings? Do you use sports, work, or sex as a way of avoiding your feelings?

8 Would you enjoy being more expressive and creative with yourself?

9 Do you feel that you can discipline yourself so as to lead a healthier, happier life?

10 How would you like to express yourself more creatively?

Affirmations for the Throat Chakra

I am able to harness my will power to control addictive influences in my life.

I am ready to put my negative habits to one side and openly develop my creativity.

I substitute love, joy, and creative expression for old patterns of addiction and abuse.

I willingly give up (smoking, alcohol abuse, dope, overeating and unhealthy dieting) to enhance my own creative gifts.

Love opens the door for me to feel whole and complete.

Everything I do is an expression of love.

It is now safe for me to express my feelings.

I love and trust my creative gifts.

It is now right for me to express the best of who I am now.

I release the fear and doubts which block the way to my creative expression.

I am confident in the healing power of love to open my throat for greater self-expression.

The Brow Chakra

Element: beyond the Throat Chakra elements are no longer associated with chakras

Archetype: Athena, goddess of wisdom and judgment

Sense: inner vision

Shape: a star

Sound: "Om" (to be chanted into the Brow Chakra)

Soul lesson: detachment and intuition

The Brow Chakra is often referred to in esoteric teaching as the Third Eye. It is located behind the nose at the level of the brow. It stimulates the pituitary gland which channels energy into the physical body and governs both growth and coordination.

The Brow Chakra gives insight and intuition; it also permits a person to master spiritual and emotional growth, transformation and, ultimately, death. It is believed that through a lifetime of rigorous practice, focusing on the development of this chakra, Tibetan lamas can actually control the moment of their death. The Brow Chakra also governments intelligence, perception, and wisdom. At its purest and most fully functional it reflects Divine Wisdom. When it is partially developed it reflects intellectual ideas, theories, and ideologies. At a deep level it links the small egoistic mind to a greater cosmic consciousness. We sense this as an experience of completeness, a feeling of oneness with the Source. At this level of awareness there is no duality, only a sense of unity and communion.

Through the Brow Chakra we are able to open ourselves to universal, creative energy. This allows us to direct ourselves consciously towards the fulfillment of our life's purpose. The secret of the great masters lies in their ability to focus their attention in this center in order to channel their visions into a physical reality.

Enlightenment

The height of creativity comes about when the mind, emotions, and physical body resonate harmoniously with one another. The mind then has the fullest potential for creative manifestation. Most people choose to identify their small minds as the source of their being and not look further into the vast realm of creation for the source of life energy. Given such intensified awareness there can be unlimited energy and unlimited creativity.

Thought can be creative and healing. When we give ourselves the possibility of creating our lives the way we want them to be, we tap into a vast reserve of energy. Through our imagination and creative abilities we can build, create, and manifest our intentions to lead a healthy, fulfilling, and happy life.

When the Brow Chakra is awakened it gives conscious control over every cell in the body. In this way we can open ourselves to healing. This enhances our vibrational quality so intensely that we become like radiant suns, spreading joy wherever our light shines. It is not exaggerating to say this opening gives the very soul its outlet of expression.

Enlightenment is associated with this chakra. This is when the veil of the ego is dropped for a glimpse of the higher realms of consciousness. The perfection of the universe and the related order of all things becomes apparent in a stunningly clear way. One's own purpose may also be illuminated. People who have experienced enlightenment describe a blazing white light behind their eyes in the Brow Chakra and an intense quality of energy which vibrates throughout their bodies. Sometimes this energy is so powerful that a person's life can be completely transformed. In the East this bolt of energy is known as Shakti.

Such moments of enlightenment may be very brief, indeed lasting less than a twenty-fifth of a second. Yet within that moment all tension, fear, and doubt vanish as the certainty of one's being becomes revealed. There is a Zen saying which goes:

"Before Enlightenment I chopped wood and carried water.

After Enlightenment I chopped wood and carried water."

In other words, the practical realities of everyday life remain exactly the same. Only one's view of attitude has changed sufficiently to allow transformation to occur. Our understanding of the universe and the acceptance of our place within the scheme of things frees us. Neurotic energy can then be transformed to enhance our development and growth, and to support our healing in creative, pleasurable, and enjoyable ways.

Wisdom

The Hindi word for the Brow Chakra is Visuddhi. This means purity and comes about when the Throat Chakra becomes activated and simple human love turns into divine compassion and understanding—otherwise known as unconditional love. This is a love which raises our level of understanding above petty hurts and selfish claims. Our capacity to live in the light of unconditional love grows and the soul becomes increasingly selfless, our power of understanding widens and our minds become stronger, more receptive to positive thought. The soul begins to recognize God everywhere, even in the smallest forms of life. As Christ said: "Blessed are the pure in heart for they shall see God."

Wisdom derives from the sum total of our life experience and reflects the deepest knowing within us. It evolves and develops as we mature. The ability of the mind to stand back and detach itself from the immediate business of getting on with life allows us freedom from over-identification with our emotions and our personality. It helps reinforce our faith in the innate goodness of life and to carry on when life appears too complicated or problematic for us to see new directions or an alternate path clearly. This awareness, that we call wisdom, helps us to avoid the pitfalls which follow an ego-led existence.

The Brow Chakra has within its scope of control the ability to interpret a situation or scenario in its most positive light. Within its realm of generating energy is our ability to change negative situations into a springboard for the positive. This ability to distill wisdom from life's learning experiences is one of the primary functions of our inner sight. Such shifts of perception occur when we allow love to flow through our hearts.

To move from "This situation is horrible" to "I can learn something about myself here" is a reframing which our minds accomplish through the practice of judicious detachment. This sense of perspective in looking at our lives allows us to accumulate knowledge and understanding. The synthesis of this knowledge is wisdom and this is invaluable. As the Biblical proverb tells us, "It is far better to have wisdom than gold."

Transformation

There is a universal law that nature abhors a vacuum, and this holds for our lives as well. There is only change. We have within ourselves the ability to transform any situation, no matter how terrible, into a positive experience for ourselves. This choice is within our capacity at all times. It is a direct function of the mind which allows us to make a leap into the realm of the spirit and ennoble any situation with grace, beauty, and truth.

By the same token the mind also has the ability to sabotage or negate positive situations. Our attitudes are a focal point, reflecting back to us how we view ourselves and the world around us. If we let judgments, criticism, or past experiences forever color our actions we will grow or develop slowly and with difficulty. A person's willingness to take risks or challenge pre-existing patterns of behavior will directly transform his levels of energy. This is all the result of our thoughts and attitudes. When the mind is still and at peace our bodies function normally and easily. When our minds are agitated, our bodies cannot find rest. When our minds are agitated, our bodies reflect the same state of tension. Blood pressure changes, stomach acidity, bowel function, and menstrual cycles are all affected by tension.

The Brow Chakra if too congested will alter our clarity of perception and level of awareness. This chakra regulates our inner sense of knowing. When we tune into ourselves and listen to our inner truths we can become our own guides. Daily tasks and events become transformed by the way in which we look at things and value our own perceptions and insights.

Focusing in the Brow Center brings control and awareness. We can detach ourselves from negative thoughts and disruptive emotions.

It is said that the unconscious mind will respond to any direction that it is given. To give an illustration, the Universal Intelligences say "yes" to everything. If, for instance, you say to yourself, "I am fat and ugly and no one loves me," the Universal Intelligence will respond by saying "Yes." If you say, "I am beautiful and everybody loves me," the Universal Intelligence will say "Yes."

We get to choose which we wish to express to the world, our self-love or our self-hatred. To create our lives consciously and channel our positive vision of ourselves it is essential to know what it is we want. When we understand the basic principle of creative manifestation then we can look at the impediments which are in the way of our allowing what we want for ourselves. Our attitudes reflect our basic underlying beliefs about what life is, and if they are not positive and affirmative then they may be blocking the goodness we long for and seek. If this is so, what will work for us is to examine our fundamental underlying attitudes and life scripts either in therapy, a workshop, or with someone trusted and respected.

Another function of the Brow Chakra is the ability it gives us to look within and to reflect on the conscious mind. This can lead us to guidance and direction which may come in the form of dreams, or an inner voice. The power of intuition, when recognized and accepted, is an invaluable guiding light to our well-being and happiness.

An over-active Brow Chakra is the result of fear and doubt. Many people live primarily in their minds and thereby avoid emotions or deep feelings. The mind is dry without the connection to the love in our hearts. If fear has been a driving force in your life, then it may well be very difficult to learn to trust love, warmth, and feelings. This is a new form of learning which requires patience and care.

It takes a conscious willingness to check out reality and see if it is alright to give into our feelings and trust ourselves. The mind is the driving force of our thoughts, feelings, and sensations, and only when we can get beyond our minds can we release our fears and anxieties. When we do this, however, we experience our basic nature, which is freedom itself.

Movements for the Brow Chakra
Choose music that is still and detached. Baroque music or anything slow is ideal to move to.

1 Perhaps the single bet movement for the Brow Chakra is to do nothing! This chakra tends to be so over-active in most people that it is often best to find a relaxing, semi-supine position and to rest. In the Alexander Technique there is a wonderful exercise which I often recommend to people. It consists of lying down in a semi-supine position and resting or meditating for twenty minutes. The semi-supine position is lying on your back with your knees up and your feet flat on the floor. It requires a hard surface beneath you so that gravity can work for you to release the spine and help the whole back relax. I suggest you put a book 3 inches thick under your occiput bones at the back of your head. This allows your whole spine to be flat and takes the stress of your back and your neck.

2 Put your hands on to your hips with your elbows as far apart from your body as they will go. This helps to flatten the back muscles. Breathe deeply several times to release any superficial tension you may be holding. Let your tongue fall back into the back of your throat and let your eyes fall back into their sockets.

3 Twenty minutes of this a day will help the spine straighten itself our. It will let the spongy material between the discs fill with spinal fluid. It gives a wonderful, relaxed sense of calm and well-being. It calms the mind and aids tranquillity.

Massage for the Brow Chakra

As there is often so much tension in the head this massage is deeply soothing and relaxing. Make sure that you and your partner are both comfortable and warm. Make a peaceful environment by lighting a candle, burning incense and, perhaps, playing gentle, calming music.

1 Start the massage by asking your partner to take several deep breaths. Ask them to let their eyes fall back into their sockets and the tongue fall back into the back of their throat to release tension. Ask them to release their jaw and chin so it is loose and free.

2 Sit behind your partner so that you can easily touch the top of their head and face. Begin by placing your fingers gently on the temporal bones beside the eyes. Keep your touch feather-light. This is a place where tension accumulates and by simply placing your hands there your partner will begin to unwind and relax. Do this for approximately five minutes. Make sure that you are relaxed and free of tension as you can transfer this tension to your partner. This is a moment for meditation and peaceful thoughts.

3 When you feel that your partner is starting to relax, begin by drawing energy from the Third Eye area between the brows. Make clockwise circles and pull the energy up and out. Flick it away. Burn a candle and incense to purify the energy. Do this for approximately five minutes.

4 Massage the forehead (using the fingertips of your right hand) back and forth across the Brow. Anchor your left hand on the neck or shoulder to maintain polarity. Be

gentle and communicate with your partner to see if your touch, tempo, and pressure is agreeable. Do this for fifteen minutes. Your partner may fall asleep. They will become deeply relaxed. Often people will snore or fall into a deep relaxation.

The Color of the Brow Chakra

The color which relates to the Brow Chakra is indigo blue, the color of universal healing. Blue is the most used color in the world today. It soothes and tranquilizes, is a good antidote to violence, anger, or aggression, and can be used to cool inflammations and eruptions.

Too much blue in a person's aura signifies they live too much in the mental sphere. They may need magnetizing or touching to help them reconnect with their physical surroundings. "Blue people" are often powerful healers and have a calm and soothing perspective. They have the ability to detach themselves from any aggressive atmosphere or environment and lend harmony, tranquillity, and clarity to a situation. Their energy tends to help others. "Blue people" have a stillness and calmness about them. They are composed, quiet people with a natural ability to make others feel good. They are often big and gentle and can install calm and well-being in any situation.

Healing Uses for the Color Indigo Blue

It is good for:
Clarity
Releasing negative mind patterns
Promoting inspiration
Soothing inflammations
Relaxing nervous and agitated people
Soothing over-active minds
Pain relief
Respiratory depressant
Thyroid depressant
Parathyroid stimulation

Attributes of the Brow Chakra

Positive	*Negative*
Intuition	Coldness
Knowingness	Intellectualism
Wisdom	Unfeeling
Perception	Mean
Psychic healing	Tight
Telepathy	Ungracious
Empathy	Bitter
Spirituality	
Idealism	

Gemstones
Sapphire
Moonstone
Sodalite
Lapis Lazuli
Azurite
Siberian Quartz

Aromas
Jonqui
Camphor
Blue Chamomile
Eucalyptus
Melissa
Elemi

Questionnaire for the Brow Chakra

1 Do you feel that your difficulties and struggles have a purpose?

2 Do you feel your life has meaning?

3 Do you stay open to new ideas and let yourself experience new situations?

4 Do you allow yourself the opportunity to reflect on your life and the situations and relationships you have experienced?

5 Do you value your perceptions and insights?

6 Do you trust your intuition?

7 Are you willing to develop your intuitive skills as a valid means of ascertaining information and knowledge which may be useful to you?

8 Are you willing to alter your perceptions of situations and people to be more loving and accepting of them?

9 Are you willing to take responsibility for your life and create what you want for health and happiness?

10 Can you think of ten things you'd like to change in your life?

11 Can you replace these with a vision of what you would like to have?

Affirmations for the Brow Chakra

I think positive thoughts about myself and everything around me.

I open myself to my intuition and deepest knowing.

I acknowledge I am the source in creating my life the way I would like it to be.

I accept that I am an unlimited being and that I can create anything I want.

I focus on what I love and draw it to me.

I release all the impediments which block my growth and development.

I am open to new ideas, people, and situations which will enhance my joy and happiness.

I live in the truth of my grace, beauty, and intelligence.

I am responsible for the quality of love and happiness in my life.

I rethink all negative thoughts about myself and others and change them to positive energy.

I create clarity and unlimited vision for myself about my life.

I trust whatever comes to me is for my greatest joy and highest good.

The Crown Chakra

Archetype: Shaman/Guru/Buddha

Sense: a pervading peace

Shape: a scull cap which sits over the crown

Sound: "Hu" (to be chanted into the Crown Chakra)

Soul lesson: to be at one with the Source

The Crown Chakra represents the most purified and evolved level of energy in the human energy system. It is the center of spirituality, refinement, and beauty. In Yoga this center is referred to as the Thousand Petalled Lotus. This center joins the realm of physical activity to those of both mental and emotional perception and awareness, unifying all three levels. It stimulates expansion towards the development of a universal consciousness. When this center opens we received universal energy which guides us on our path and allows our true destiny to unfold.

The Crown Center is delicate. Opening it should be treated with caution. In babies it is wide open and a certain amount of growth and development is required before this center becomes stabilized; usually within the first six months of life the Crown Chakra becomes focused. It begins to close with the fontanels of the skull.

Prayer and meditation are ways in which this chakra can be opened. It may take years of practice and spiritual devotion before it is fully functional. Our spiritual evolution is dependent upon the degree to which we surrender our small and limited ego to a protective and guiding force which moves us through life.

The Crown Chakra affects the nervous system, muscle system, skin, and skeletal structure. On its most subtle level it is the seat of human consciousness. The energy from this chakra feeds and nurtures the entire person.

Struggle and Surrender

Universal energy becomes individualized and anchored in the body at this center. Our attitudes, values, and ethics will deeply reflect our connection to Universal Intelligence. If we are cut off from a spiritual dimension we will operate on limited energy and strength. This is because we have invested our life-force into our egos. Our individual egos then need to supply us with all our energy and this self-imposed limitation is what we experience as a struggle.

When we open to a Source higher than our own small, limited egos we begin to move from a lighter, freer, more energized place within ourselves. Our capacity to open to the Source is innate and built into our energetic systems. We control our own destinies through the choices we make for having and accepting love into our lives. As we surrender more and more to this Source of love operating within us we become vibrant, radiant, and happy beings.

A spiritual understanding of life will always pose certain questions for us. We may want to know the answers to such questions as: "Who am I?", "What is the purpose of my life?", "What is love?". These questions are worth serious contemplation because they offer us the possibility to reflect on our true nature. As we begin to align ourselves with higher values we will start to live in harmony with the Universal Spirit.

These questions can then have answers which we experience from the very depth of our being.

Our attitudes attract to us the people, experiences, and situations which make up our lives. These attitudes reflect back our deepest and often unconscious views of how life is or should be. Our attitudes to ourselves and to life in general are constantly being mirrored back to us. Our highest powers of perception and awareness can change the way we think about life and can change the qualitative reality of our existence. Caroline Myss, the well-known spiritual teacher, calls this "Character Power." It is a very real quality and reflects our strength and spirit in living our lives. From this chakra we radiate love which nourishes our self-esteem, inner peace, well-being, and our capacity for happiness. The more love we allow into our lives through opening our awareness to the Source of life the more love we will then have to give out in all areas of our lives.

The very nature of the Crown Chakra is to be receptive. Our willingness to receive love in the form of energy differentiates a spiritual person from one tied to the "doingness" of ego energy. People on the spiritual path learn to accept and respect the mysteries of life's ever-unfolding patterns. Those attached to the go battle with taming life and tailoring it to suit their needs and desires.

A distinguishing feature of the Crown Chakra is the capacity it gives for acceptance. When we accept ourselves and our gifts we begin to find peace within. Although we consciously create from the Brow Chakra we are asked to embrace our lives with a sense of acceptance. This process is known as surrender.

We have within our hearts the ability to heal all our own wounds and the wounds of those we love. This comes from our capacity for unconditional love. It is part of each person's destiny at some point in their life to open to the Source of life which is channeled through the Crown Chakra.

We are asked to do more than just accept our fate. We are offered the possibility of embracing our lives passionately, to love ourselves fully, and to surrender our small and petty egos to a higher Source of Self than we could possibly grasp in our limited everyday existence.

We can live predominantly from whichever chakra we choose. Life can be a constant struggle with elemental conflicts, clashes with authority or conflict with our own incarnation. We may, for example, see the business of life as the acquisition of power, money, and sexual conquest. As we move into higher realms of expressing our personal power we confront issues of love, self-worth, and inner peace.

Self-expression may be a path which we choose to explore. The mystery of our lives may be a path we wish to follow. Yet without an all-encompassing overview of life and an acceptance of who we are on all levels we will miss out on any real sense of our wholeness and completeness. We are, by our very nature, spirit in form. This asks to be recognized and is the essential quality which allows us to transform pain and struggle into a meaningful and positive dividend of our life experiences. If we fail to grasp the significance of all our efforts and endeavors, then we are also bound to miss the beauty which is available to us from this realm of the spirit.

Spiritual Energy

Within each of us there is the possibility of becoming our own unique guide to understanding and dealing with life's perplexities. We have only to tune into our own spiritual nature to know what is the best path to follow on our quest for love, understanding, and wisdom.

We may choose to project our spirituality onto a teacher or guru in order to enhance our understanding of our spiritual nature. It may even be teachings from a non-physical entity that channels information to serve as guidance and sustenance for us in times of difficulties and stress. It may appear in the guise of angels or spirit guides.

Whatever form this projection of Higher Self takes, it is, at root, an aspect of our own spiritual nature. There is nothing which is separate from the Self. All the physical and non-physical forms our mind creates, in order that we may know and understand the God force within each of us, are there to be re-absorbed back into the Self.

I met my teacher H. L. W. Poonja at a time in my life when I was troubled and perplexed by the degree of suffering I saw in myself and those of my clients suffering from abuse issues. Fate sent a messenger in the form of a young homeopath who told me about his teacher in India. I made the decision to visit Poonja. Within days of being with him all of my doubts, questions, and fears disappeared. He offered me the grace of his love and radiance; energy which helped me turn my awareness inward to the foundation of my soul. He suggested that I could identify with the bedrock of the sea or with the turbulence of the waves. he said, "If you become the substratum you are at peace. If you become the surface you are disturbed." He said, "Our desire to be free comes from freedom itself. It burns away all desires. It comes from consciousness itself." He told me this most important of his teachings: "You don't have to attain that state. You are that state. Peace is the think to look for. Think on what is permanent. The mind has expectations of what it thinks of as perfect rather than just letting whatever happens from God be perfect. What cannot be accepted or rejected is to be known, that is real. No thought, no desire, no search, just be. Be alert, watch the mind. This is freedom. Spirituality is not to accept or reject. Be with things with love. They are you. Accept them as your own self. You'll become whole living with everything as it is—I am all. All this is myself."

The Crown Chakra represents the highest aspect of the Self. When spiritual energy is suppressed many diseases can occur. They may appear through the skin, nerves, or emotions. There are many stress-related illnesses which occur because we fail to honor the spiritual aspects of our lives. It is through the opening of the Crown Chakra that we truly learn the most important lesson—that of surrendering to the Source.

Movements for the Crown Chakra
Choose music that is soft, gentle, and has a spiritual quality. A Gregorian chant is good to move to.

1 Lying on your back, head pointing towards the north, with your knees up and your feet on the floor, begin to breathe gently and deeply. Imagine that you are drawing air in from the top of your head. Begin to relax and let go of tension. As you exhale, imagine that toxins and tension are moving out through the soles of your feet. Repeat this

exercise for approximately 20 minutes. It is a yogic breathing exercise which releases deep toxins from your auric field. It takes concentration and imagination.

2   Ask a friend to cradle your head gently with their hands, lightly holding your skull. The longer they hold your head the stronger the Cranio-Sacral pulse becomes. The opening and contracting rhythms of this pulse help you to relax, become receptive, and feel at ease. Focus your attention on releasing tension and expanding your awareness. Take 15–20 minutes to enjoy this exercise.

Massage for the Crown Chakra

Sit quietly with your partner's head cradled in your hands. Working with the delicate energy of the Crown Chakra requires that you be very gentle and sensitive. It is important that you create a warm and peaceful atmosphere. Light a candle, burn incense, and play soft music. Make sure your partner is warm and comfortable.

1   Hold your partner's head lightly in your hands until they start to feel comfortable and relaxed.

2   Gently begin to draw energy out of the Crown Chakra, using the fingers of your right hand moving in a clockwise direction. Do this for 2–3 minutes. You need less time for this chakra than for the others because of its sensitive nature.

3   Gently rub the crown of the head with the palm of your right hand, holding the base of the head with your left hand. You may make figures of eight, small circles, or simply rub back and forth. Do this for 5–8 minutes.

The Color of the Crown Chakra

The color of the Crown Chakra is violet. This is the shortest wave of light ray in the visible spectrum and is a motor depressant, depressing all active parts of the body except the spleen and the parathyroid. This color will relax, calm, and depress the nerves of overly excited people. It acts as an antibiotic, building protective organisms which destroy their harmful counterparts.

Violet also has the fastest vibration in the visible spectrum. It relates to purple, being its spiritual aspect. Purple is a strong color and principally relates to power. For instance, the robes of royalty and high-ranking church officials are purple. Historically it is a color which was reserved for only the highest ranking and most powerful of people because it was a difficult color to manufacture, requiring effort and expense.

One of the gemstones for the Crown Chakra widely used today to instill a spiritual quality in one's life is amethyst. This stone carries violet energies and helps to calm and mind and restore harmony and overcome imbalance.

Healing Uses for the Color Violet

It is good for:
Sores and ulcers of the skin
Nervous and mental disorders
Neurosis
Neuralgia
Sciatica
Scalp diseases
Epilepsy
Concussions
Rheumatism
Kidney and bladder weakness
Alcoholism

Attributes of the Crown Chakra

Positive   *Negative*
Spirituality   Despair
Service   Destructiveness
Faith   Alcoholism
Peace   Epilepsy
Refinement   Egoism
Beauty
Communion
Joy
Gratitude

Gemstones
Amethyst
Diamond
Quartz crystal
Pearl
Alexandrite

Aromas
Lavender
Elemi
Violet
Clary Sage

Questionnaire for the Crown Chakra

1 Does your life have a spiritual dimension?
2 Do you have faith that life is good?
3 Do you feel that your life has a particular purpose?
4 Do you cling to the past and resist change?
5 Do you believe that joy, beauty, and grace are within the realm of possibility for you?
6 How do you look at the problems and situations in your life? Can you see them within a spiritual context or do you feel a victim of circumstances?
7 Are you open to receive your highest good and greatest joy?
8 Can you detach yourself from the script of your life and begin to see a wider vision of yourself?
9 Can you accept that deep at your core you are divinely protected and guided?
10 Do you give thanks for the opportunities life gives you?
11 Do you rejoice in your being?

Affirmations for the Crown Chakra

I am open and receptive to all life.

Love is eternal.

Love makes me free.

I am willing to go beyond my limitations to express and experience greater joy.

I am always willing to take the next step in my life.

I am divinely protected and guided.

I am safe and all life loves and supports me now.

Love surrounds me, protects and nourishes me.

I go beyond limiting beliefs and accept myself totally.

I acknowledge that the source of love is within me.

I am willing to be responsible for the quality of love and joy I have in my life.

The more love I give the more there is to receive.

I am open to the goodness and abundance of the Universe.

BOOKS BY THE CROSSING PRESS

Healing with Astrology
By Marcia Starck

Bring balance and energy to your life using the correspondences between your horoscope and a wide range of natural healing systems.

$14.95 • Paper • ISBN 0-89594-862-1

Healing with Chinese Herbs
By Lesley Tierra

Tierra lists the properties and therapeutic uses of over one hundred herbs.

$14.95 • Paper • ISBN 0-89594-829-X

Healing with Color Zone Therapy
By Joseph Corvo and Lilian Verner-Bonds

Corvo and Verner-Bonds introduce a form of therapy that treats the whole person: the physical, the emotional, and the spiritual.

$14.95 • Paper • ISBN 0-89594-925-3

Healing with Flower and Gemstone Essences
By Diane Stein

Instructions for choosing and using flowers and gems are combined with descriptions of their effect on emotional balance.

$14.95 • Paper • ISBN 0-89594-856-7

Healing with Gemstones and Crystals
By Diane Stein

Details on how to choose and use the Earth's precious gems are supplemented by explanations of the significance of this type of healing.

$14.95 • Paper • ISBN 0-89594-831-1

To receive a current catalog from The Crossing Press
please call toll-free, 800-777-1048.
Visit our Web site on the Internet: www. crossingpress.com